Beyond Statistics
A Practical Guide to Data Analysis

Benjamin Miller
Salem State College

Allyn and Bacon
Boston London Toronto Sydney Tokyo Singapore

Contents

v

To the memory of Paul David Miller

Preface

What is data analysis?

Data analysis is more than statistics. It is the entire process of finding out what happened, of turning data into conclusions and questions for future research. This process includes entering data into a computer, checking the data for errors and omissions, deciding what statistics we want to compute, what graphs we want to draw, what tests we want to perform (if any), and figuring out how to arrange our data to make it possible for the computer to do these things. Until they have done it, most people have no idea how much work is involved in these non-statistical aspects of data analysis. That's where this book comes in.

About the book

The first three chapters provide some important background and introduce some important terminology. Each of the remaining chapters deals with a different aspect of data analysis: data entry, data cleaning, arranging (and rearranging) data, creating new variables, combining data, displaying data, and collapsing data. Each of these chapters (4 - 10) explains why, when, and how a particular set of data techniques is used. The chapters include many illustrations, using small sets of (mostly) made-up data. Between some of the chapters are larger-scale demonstrations, using real data. In all cases the data are provided on the Allyn & Bacon web site (www.abacon.com/miller), and you should replicate the demonstration using your statistical software. Finally, the later chapters include both pencil-and-paper and computer exercises.

About statistics

The purpose of this book is to help you apply your knowledge of statistics to the kinds of problems you are likely to encounter in research. Although we will talk about statistics, this book is not about statistics; it is about data. If you have taken (or are now taking) an introductory course in statistics, you understand central tendency, variability, probability, hypothesis testing, and the like, but you may not have a very good idea what to do with a boxful (or a diskful) of data. How do you get data into a computer? What do you do with them once they're in? This book will show you.

About statistical software

To some people statistical software makes perfect sense and to others it is a perfect nightmare. In my experience, trouble with statistical software usually comes from asking "What should I do?" or "How do I work this?" rather than "What do I want to do?" Remember that the computer (and the statistical software it is running) is only a tool; you are the brains of the operation. It is up to you to say, clearly and precisely and in English, what you want to do. If you do this, it is not hard to find the right menu or command in your particular statistical software.

This book will help you with the process of thinking about your research questions and figuring out how to get answers to them out of your data using statistical software. The book is not, however, a software manual. Thinking about what to do is the same for everyone, but ultimately the question of how to do it depends on what software you are using. We will talk about software in general, but for help with your particular software you'll want a manual or an expert.

Because different readers will be using different software, all the examples use an imaginary program that understands commands given in a quasi-English known as pseudocode. Computer scientists use pseudocode when they are concerned with showing what a program does rather than how it is written. Pseudocode uses a minimum of special terms or syntax; it attempts to convey, tersely but plainly, what we are asking the computer to do.

The key to data analysis is not remembering a thousand rules for a thousand situations, but having a few good habits. I hope this book will help you learn those habits.

■ ■ ■

My father taught me at a tender age to be methodologically orthodox and pedagogically radical, and I hope this book lives up to that credo. Meanwhile I have many wise and sympathetic people to thank.

A backpacking companion is the ultimate captive audience, and Alec Bodkin provided miles of listening and encouragement when I was trying to figure out what it was I needed to write. A Summer faculty writing workshop sponsored by Salem State College was the perfect opportunity to begin putting something on paper. I am indebted to my workshop colleagues – Joe Buttner, Kristine Doll, Eileen Margerum, Eric Metchik, Nancy Schultz, and J.D. Scrimgeour – for their careful reading, their bulls-eye questions and their creative suggestions. Norman Miller, Sue Regan, and Jeffrey Adams read later drafts and offered many invaluable suggestions. My brother Paul died before I could properly thank him for his many contributions, but in substance and style the finished book bears the imprint of his sharp eye and keen judgment. Mindy Clawson worked magic to turn a big mess of words and figures into a book, improving it substantially in the process. Becky Pascal, at Allyn & Bacon, was unfailingly helpful and patient. Very patient.

Orientation

Chapter Outline

1. It is important to distinguish between variables, values, and constants.

2. There are many distinctions among different types of variables. Some of the most useful distinctions are:

    a. Independent and dependent variables.

    b. Discrete and continuous variables.

    c. Categorical and quantitative variables.

3. There are four broad categories of questions we can ask about data:

    a. Questions about the distribution of a single variable.

    b. Questions about differences between groups or conditions.

    c. Questions about the association between categorical variables.

    d. Questions about the relation between quantitative variables.

4. There are several principles that make data analysis easier, more fun, and less error-prone.

    a. Frame questions in terms of data rather than in terms of software.

    b. Look at the data before computing anything; be alert for errors, outliers, skewed distributions, and so on.

    c. Don't do categorical things with quantitative variables or quantitative things with categorical variables.

ONE OF THE MOST significant problems that we encounter in learning to analyze data is knowing what to do in different data situations. The statistics text offers us false security: If Chapter 8 is about t-tests and Chapter 9 is about analysis of variance, we can be reasonably confident in choosing a t-test for the Chapter 8 problems and in choosing analysis of variance for the Chapter 9 problems. But when the exam comes along and the different kinds of problems are mixed together we often make mistakes. Real data analysis is more like the exam than like the problems at the end of the chapter.

This chapter offers a solution to the what-should-I-do problem in the form of a simple framework for talking about data and asking questions about data.

1.1   Variables, values, and constants

variables &
constants

Let's begin with some important – and probably familiar – terminology. A *variable* is, not surprisingly, something that varies. A *constant*, on the other hand, is something that does not vary. Temperature is something that varies in a pretty obvious way, so temperature is a variable. But in Mammoth Cave the temperature is 54°F year round, so temperature there is a constant. There's no contradiction here; the point is that we can say what's a variable and what's a constant only within a specific context.

Suppose, for example, you are interested in the (possible) relation between obesity and hypertension. You go out and find a few hundred people and weigh them and measure their blood pressure. You now have a set of data containing two variables: weight and blood pressure. But you realize that weight alone doesn't tell the whole story: someone 5'2" tall who weighs 200 pounds is probably obese, but someone 6'2" tall who weighs 200 pounds is probably not. Height is a variable that you care about, but since you didn't measure it it's not a variable in your data. Accordingly, you might repeat your study, selecting only people who are, say, 5'10" tall. Now your data set contains the same two variables as before (weight and blood pressure), but height is no longer an extraneous variable; in this new context it is a constant.

Any variable can be turned into a constant simply by not allowing it to vary, and that's about all there is to know about constants. Variables, on the other hand, are what research is all about, and there are a few things to know about variables. Let's look at some (hypothetical) blood pressure data:

```
name        weight      blood pressure
Ed          153         130
Ted         175         120
Ned         240         110
Fred        192         150
Jed         132         170
Hubert      147         140
...
```

variables &
values

Each row contains the name, weight and blood pressure measurements of a particular subject, or *case*. Each column contains a *variable*, something that varies from case to case. Each item is a *value* of a particular variable for a particular case. Thus Jed is the value of the variable name for the fifth case; 240 is the value of the variable weight in the case of Ned; and 120 is the value of the variable blood pressure in the case of Ted. The difference between a variable and a value is very important because, as we will see in the next section, we make a number of distinctions among variables in terms of the kind of values they have.

1.2   Kinds of variables

Independent
variables
correspond to
groups,
conditions,
predictors.

There are many distinctions among variables. In this section we will look at three that are particularly important: independent/dependent, discrete/continuous, and categorical/-quantitative.

Independent and dependent variables. This is a familiar if not always easy distinction. For example, if we give group A an anti-anxiety drug and group B a placebo and then measure everybody's anxiety levels, the *treatment* variable (drug/placebo) is an independent variable and the *outcome* variable (anxiety) is a dependent variable. One way to know which is which is to notice that we (sometimes) manipulate the independent variable (in this case by deciding which drug(s) to use), but we never manipulate the dependent vari-

Dependent
variables
correspond to
results.

able. Another way is to think of the value of the dependent variable as depending on the value of the independent variable; in this case how much anxiety someone has may depend on which treatment group we put her in. Which variable is independent and which is dependent is usually fairly clear, but not always. If we ask people their political party and who they voted for in the last election, vote is more likely to depend on party than the other way around. But what if we ask people their position on abortion rights and their position on affirmative action? Here there does not seem to be a plausible independent/dependent distinction.

Discrete and continuous variables. The engine in your car can have 3 cylinders or 4 cylinders but it can't have 3.1 cylinders. Number of cylinders is a discrete variable: between two adjacent values (e.g. 3 and 4 cylinders) on the scale there cannot be any intermediate value (e.g. 3.5 cylinders). By contrast, your engine can get 35 or 36 miles per gallon, or it can get 35.1 mpg, or 35.11 or 35.111 or 35.1111... Miles per gallon is a continuous variable: no matter how close two measurements are, it is always possible for a third measurement to fall between them.[1] Notice that the discrete/continuous distinction gets blurry at the edges: If you weigh people using a digital scale that rounds weights to the nearest pound, then you are measuring something (weight) that is inherently continuous using a scale of measurement that is artificially discrete. You can't turn a discrete variable into a continuous one, but you can turn a continuous variable into a discrete one. As you will see, we often do this in analyzing data.

> *Discrete variables count things and events.*

> *Continuous variables measure.*

Categorical and quantitative variables. The distinction between *categorical* and *quantitative* variables is important because what we can do with one kind is so different from what we can do with the other. Height, weight, number of cavities, shoe size, age, and income are all quantitative variables; the kind of measuring they do is to quantify. Some quantities can be measured on continuous scales (height, weight) and others are discrete (number of cavities), but in both cases we are measuring a quantity of something. Quantitative variables ask *How many?* (discrete) or *How much?* (continuous), while categorical variables ask *Which?*

> *Categorical variables classify.*

> *Quantitative variables count and measure.*

There are two kinds of categorical variable. Political party, sex, zip code, species, and marital status are all *nominal* categorical variables. Nominal, from the Latin *nomen* (name) refers to the fact that the values of such variables are names (of categories); the kind of measuring they do is to categorize, or classify. You are either female or male; married or not; you belong to one political party or another, and so on. You can't be something in between, and one category isn't more or less than another.

> *Nominal categorical variables name.*

On the other hand, variables such as position on the bestseller list, critics' ratings of movies or restaurants (★, ★★, ★★★, etc.), or finishing place in a race are *ordinal* categorical variables. These variables measure by categorizing, but the categories they use can be ordered. The values of ordinal variables are not only names of categories, they are ranks or comparative judgments. For example, if my self-help book, *Living with Boring Neighbors: A Survivor's Guide,* is no. 3 on the bestseller list, we know something about how well it is selling, but only relatively. It might be selling much better than the no. 4 book, or only a little better; it might have sold a million copies last week, or a dozen. It is very important to keep in mind that ordinal variables express *only* order. Even though ranks are expressed by numbers, these are not numbers that count or measure in the usual sense, and you can't do quan-

> *Ordinal categorical variables order, rank or rate.*

---

[1] Discrete variables are sometimes referred to as counting variables, because their values are always integers (counting numbers), and continuous variables are sometimes referred to as measuring variables, but these terms are ambiguous and potentially misleading. For some purposes, counting is legitimately considered a kind of measurement.

titative things — such as computing a mean[2] — with these numbers.

1.3   Kinds of questions

Most research questions fall into one of four broad categories. Determining which category we're working in goes a long way toward deciding what kinds of procedures are (and aren't) appropriate. The flow chart below summarizes the relations between types of data, types of questions, and types of procedures. The tables and graphs mentioned in this section are discussed in detail in chapters 8 and 9.

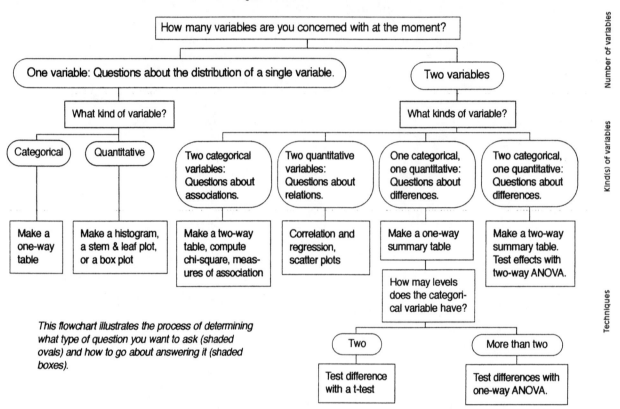

This flowchart illustrates the process of determining what type of question you want to ask (shaded ovals) and how to go about answering it (shaded boxes).

This chart is not everything there is to know about analyzing data. Rather, it will point you in the right direction when you have some data and don't know what to do with them.

Questions about a distribution. Often we have questions about the distribution of a single variable, either categorical or quantitative. For example, a teacher who has given a multiple-choice exam has some questions about how the scores are distributed: what is the mean? the standard deviation? the range? He may want to know the shape of the distribution (is it skewed? flat? normal? multimodal?) and whether there are any extremely high or low scores (outliers) that may be pulling the mean up or down. In addition to computing the various descriptive statistics mentioned, one way to answer some of these questions is to plot a *histogram*, or *grouped frequency distribution*.

---

[2] There is no practical difficulty in computing the mean of an ordinal variable, but interpreting the result is another story. The problem is that the intervals between ranks do not necessarily represent the same amount of difference between the things ranked. The difference between \$1 and \$2 is the same amount of money as the difference between \$2 and \$3, and so on. But the difference betwen first place and second place in a race might be .02 seconds while the difference between second and third place might be 5 seconds. The mean is defined as the value of μ such that $\sum (X - \mu) = 0$, and this definition is violated by variables that do not have equal intervals.

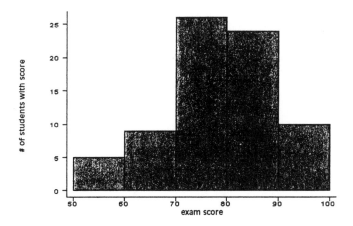

a histogram, or grouped frequency distribution

Histograms show the number of cases (here, students) falling within defined ranges of the variable (test score). The pattern of bar heights is the shape of the distribution of test scores. Another way to see the shape of the distribution is with a *box-and-whisker plot* (described in detail in Chapter 9).

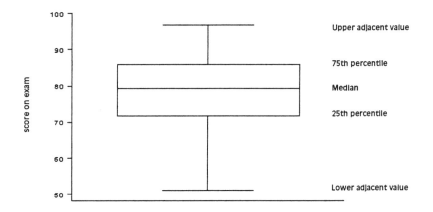

a box-and-whisker plot

The teacher might also want to know the distribution of answers to a particular multiple-choice question, such as:

> 17. Napoleon Bonaparte was born in
>   a. Corsica
>   b. Corfu
>   c. Sardinia
>   d. Paris
>   e. Jersey City

Knowing what percentage of his students chose each answer will tell him something about what they learned and didn't learn. For this he would use a frequency table:

```
Question 17
     choice  |   Freq.    Percent
-------------|----------------------
          A  |     52      69.33
          B  |      8      10.67
          C  |     14      18.67
          D  |     12      16.00
          E  |      1       1.33
-------------|----------------------
     Total   |     75     100.00
```

A frequency table shows the number (frequency) of scores at each level of the independent variable.

Or consider a pediatrician measuring a child's height. To determine whether the child is growing at an appropriate rate she needs to be able to compare the child's height to a distribution of the heights of a large number of children of the same age and sex. If she can assume the distribution is normal (there is a test for this) then she can turn the child's height into a standard (z) score and then into a percentile. If the child's height is at the 40th percentile but was at the 80th percentile a year ago, clearly the child's growth has slowed; something may be wrong.

Finally, suppose a gubernatorial candidate running on an education reform platform argues that the school day must be lengthened. To strengthen his rhetoric he points out that the average school day length is only five and a half hours. Because you've learned not to believe anything he says you seek to verify (or discredit) his claim. You call a random sample of 100 school districts around the state and ask them all how long their school day is. Your data will allow you to compute a t-test of the hypothesis that the average school day length is 5.5 hours.

Questions about differences. A great deal of research asks questions about differences between groups or conditions (values, or levels, of a categorical independent variable) in terms of some quantitative dependent measure. For example, if we look at the difference in reading test scores (quantitative dependent variable) between students taught in a six-hour school day and students taught in an eight-hour day (levels of a categorical independent variable), we can measure the differences with means and standard deviations and present these in a summary table, or table of means.

> *A summary table shows the mean, s.d., and frequency of the scores at each level of the independent variable.*

```
                 ┊ Summary of reading test score
  day length     ┊ Mean     s.d.    N
-----------------┊-----------------------------
     6 hours     ┊ 48.4     27.9    10
     8 hours     ┊ 59.7     31.5    10
-----------------┊-----------------------------
       Total     ┊ 54.1     29.5    20
```

We can also present the difference in a bar graph, which conveys less information but makes the point more clearly:

> *A bar graph shows the mean (y-axis) of the scores at each level of the independent variable (x-axis).*

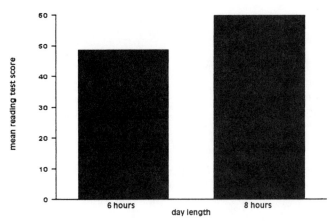

We may use a two-sample t-test to evaluate the possibility that the difference arose by chance (i.e. through sampling error). If we can reject this possibility, we may be able to predict that a school with a six-hour day could raise test scores by lengthening the day to eight hours, but we could not predict that the school could raise test scores even more by lengthening the day to ten hours because this level of the independent variable (day length) wasn't sampled in the experiment.

Questions about associations. A huge amount of research asks about whether two (or more) categorical variables are associated with one another. For example, we may have some data on school day length (six hours or less and more than six hours) and reading test scores (at or below median and above median). Notice that although day length and test scores are both inherently quantitative, here they have been measured using categorical variables. We would cross-tabulate day length (short/long) and test scores (high/low):

```
                    test scores
day length  │ ≤ median    > median
────────────┼──────────────────────
 ≤ 6 hours  │    60          40
 > 6 hours  │    45          55
```

A cross-tabulation shows the number of cases in each combination of two categorical variables.

A table shows the number (frequency) of cases (here, school districts) that fall into each of the combinations of values of two categorical values. This table shows that schools with long days are more likely than short-day schools to have high test scores. If necessary we could use a chi-square test to try to rule out the possibility that our result came about by chance. This would allow us to predict that other long-day schools have a certain likelihood of having high test scores.

Questions about relations. In the previous section I use *association*, somewhat arbitrarily, to refer to a contingency between two categorical variables, but when the same question concerns two quantitative variables I will, again somewhat arbitrarily, use the term *relation*. For example, if we randomly sample 100 school districts and record their school day lengths and reading test scores, we may examine the relation between these variables using a scatter plot:

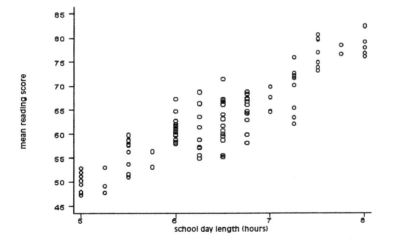

A scatter plot shows each case's values on two quantitative variables.

The pattern of the data points indicates a fairly strong linear relation between day length and reading scores. We can measure its strength and test its reliability using methods of correlation and regression, which may allow us to predict that a longer school day will raise test scores.

Each of the methods used in the preceding examples was an appropriate choice for the kind of data that were available and for the question being asked. The importance of these four basic categories – distributions, differences, associations, relations – comes from the guidance they offer in data analysis. Identifying what kind of data you have and what kind of question(s) you are asking will help you think straight about what you want to do.

1.4   Some principles of data analysis

There are a few general principles that you should keep in mind throughout this book and whenever you work with data. They will make your life easier and your work better.

Principle 1: Have a destination.   Most basic data activities are not software specific. If you know what you want to do, chances are any statistical software will do it; if you don't, no software will help you. For example, any software worth talking about will let you make a new variable that is the sum of two existing variables. The specific way of doing this will vary from package to package; for example, here are three commands that create a new variable (newvar) that is the sum of two existing variables (x1 and x2):

SAS:	newvar = x1 + x2
SPSS:	compute newvar = x1 + x2
Stata:	generate newvar = x1 + x2

You will find that these variations don't matter if you approach data analysis from the perspective of what you want to do rather than from the perspective of how the software works.

I can't say this strongly enough. The reason many people find software manuals confusing and unhelpful is that they don't quite know what they want to do. At this point in your data analysis career it is crucial that you give most of your attention and effort to thinking about what needs to be done, and why, in a particular data situation; worry about the software only enough to get your work done. I've met plenty of software whizzes who couldn't analyze data, but I've never met a competent data analyst who couldn't reasonably quickly figure out how to use a new software package to accomplish a particular task.

Principle 2: Look at the data.   Always look at the data — and I mean always — before you run tests or compute summary statistics. There may be something unanticipated or erroneous in your data that you should know about before you start blindly computing things. Carpenters live by the rule "Measure twice, cut once." The same idea applies to us: "Think twice, compute once." Why is this so important? After all, the computer is doing all the work, quickly, and we're not wasting any two-by-fours. What's the harm in a few extra computations?

Extra computations sometimes entail a subtle scientific risk. Suppose we hypothesize that taking ginkgo pills improves memory. We recruit a random sample of 20 people and randomly divide them into two groups of ten. We give all subjects a memory test, then give group A ginkgo and group B a placebo for a month. We then give all subjects another memory test, comparable to the first, and subtract the first score (pretest) from the second score (posttest) to see how much memory improvement there was. Our data look like this:

Ginkgo group	Placebo group
-5	-6
-9	-5
10	-1
7	-9
-1	1
81	10
1	4
-1	7
-6	-1
4	0

If we plunge blithely into testing our hypothesis without looking at the data, we will find that the mean memory scores for the ginkgo and placebo groups are 8.1 and 0, respectively.

Even though a t-test will show that this difference is not significant, we may nevertheless be struck by the rather large difference – a difference predicted by our hypothesis – between the groups. Unlike a Type I error, the risk here cannot be quantified. But psychologists have found many situations in which the first information we are exposed to exerts a disproportionately powerful and lasting influence on our judgment. This is one of those situations. Even without statistical significance, the fact that the first thing we see is a large difference in the "right" direction may dispose us to believe that our hypothesis is correct.

If, on the other hand, we had begun by looking at the data, we might have noticed that the ginkgo group contains one whopping outlier, a score well outside of the distribution of the other scores. If we temporarily remove the outlier we find that the mean of the ginkgo group is exactly the same as the mean of the placebo group, namely zero. But couldn't the outlier be a subject whose memory really was helped by the ginkgo? Yes, it could; but there may be other, more likely explanations. Perhaps this subject did very poorly on the pretest (was sick, didn't understand the instructions, etc.). Perhaps this subject has been doing some memory exercises. Perhaps we made a data entry error. And so on. Some of these hypotheses can be checked, and we may find an explanation for the outlier. But whether we do or not, the more important point is that by looking at the data we have been inoculated against drawing a false or premature conclusion.

Principle 3: Avoid unnatural acts with data. This is related to the "think twice, compute once" idea: Don't do categorical things with quantitative data, and don't do quantitative things with categorical data (the flowchart in 1.3 is designed to prevent this). In general, statistical software doesn't distinguish between categorical and quantitative variables, and it is willing to perform all sorts of perfectly idiotic computations. For example, suppose we have some data in which we have used 1 to represent female and 2 to represent male (a common practice, which we will discuss in chapter 3):

```
> compute mean sd of sex
variable   N     mean   s.d.
sex       100    1.43   0.495
```

Apparently the mean sex of the people in our sample is 1.43. Mean sex? How can there be such a thing?[3]

As another example, suppose we have data about the solar system:

```
> tabulate distance, period
```

---

[3] Although the idea of mean sex is meaningless, this number is not. If you have a sample of 57 females (1) and 43 males (2), the sum is (57 x 1) + (43 x 2) = 143, so the mean is 143/100 = 1.43. Subtracting the value of the lower code (1), we have .43, which is the proportion of the sample that is male. This is not a coincidence. More generally, the mean minus the lower code value equals the proportion of the sample corresponding to the upper code value. This works with any dichotomous (two-valued) variable encoded using consecutive integers (1&2, 2&3, etc.). If you use 0 and 1 you don't have to subtract, and I have occasionally found this a very convenient way to compute proportions.

| Period of Revolution | Avg dist from sun (to nearest million miles) | | | | | | | | | |
Earth Days	36	67	93	142	484	887	1783	2794	3666	Total
88	1	0	0	0	0	0	0	0	0	1
225	0	1	0	0	0	0	0	0	0	1
365	0	0	1	0	0	0	0	0	0	1
687	0	0	0	1	0	0	0	0	0	1
4333	0	0	0	0	1	0	0	0	0	1
10759	0	0	0	0	0	1	0	0	0	1
30685	0	0	0	0	0	0	1	0	0	1
60189	0	0	0	0	0	0	0	1	0	1
90465	0	0	0	0	0	0	0	0	1	1
Total	1	1	1	1	1	1	1	1	1	9

There's a nice diagonal pattern of 1s in this table. If we look at it for a while we see that the farther a planet is from the sun, the longer its period of revolution. Big deal. We could have spotted that much from the raw data, and probably more quickly:

	planet	distance	period
1.	Mercury	35.9	88
2.	Venus	67.2	225
3.	Earth	93.0	365
4.	Mars	141.6	687
5.	Jupiter	483.6	4333
6.	Saturn	886.7	10759
7.	Uranus	1783.0	30685
8.	Neptune	2794.0	60189
9.	Pluto	3666.1	90465

If we had thought about the variables a bit, and perhaps consulted the flowchart, we would have found a better way to show the relation between these variables:

A line graph, like a scatter plot, is useful for showing the relation between two quantitative variables.

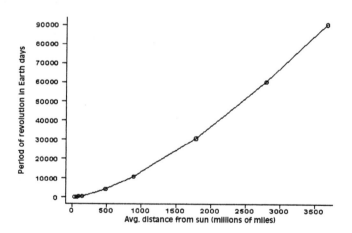

Notice that the computer does not hesitate to do things that produce output that is uninterpretable (as with mean sex) or pointless (as in the table). In short, as with any other tool, it is up to you to do the right thing.

The tools of data analysis

Chapter Outline

1. Analyzing data requires three kinds of tools:
a. tools for computing
b. tools for storing and moving data
c. statistical software

2. In spite of the apparent differences among statistical packages, all have the same basic functional components.
a. input operations
b. data editor
c. user interface
d. data manipulation tools
e. statistical computation tools
f. graphing tools
g. output operations

3. Despite the incomparable speed, power, and accuracy of computers, data analysis is and will remain a human activity.

LIKE OTHER CRAFTS, data analysis relies on tools. To analyze data we need three kinds of tools: computing tools, tools for moving and storing data, and tools for communicating with the first two.

2.1 Computing and data storage

Computing is moving symbols around according to some set of rules. The oldest computing tool is of course the brain. It's a remarkably good computing tool in some ways – it's extraordinarily flexible, it rarely breaks down, and you never have to update the operating system. However, it has very limited capacity. You can easily add four two-digit numbers using only your brain, but to multiply two four-digit numbers most of us need a pencil: there are too many intermediate results for your brain to hang on to, so you write them down. Pencil and paper vastly increase the brain's computing power by augmenting its puny working memory. This is indeed a huge bit of progress, but unfortunately the brain has two other shortcomings

the brain as computing tool

11

as a computing tool: it is slow and it is error-prone. If you use pencil and paper you can compute the average monthly rainfall in each state capitol in each of the last 100 years, but it will take a week or two and you will almost certainly make errors. The only way to speed up the brain is to use more than one. If fifty people work on the rainfall problem (e.g. one for each capitol) it will be finished much faster. Unfortunately, extra brains are expensive, and not all problems can be broken up in this way. As for errors, we can check our work or do everything twice, but this only aggravates the speed problem.

mechanical and
electronic
computing tools

Our ancient ancestors' data analysis needs were modest, and the brain-plus-writing-system was an adequate computing tool; indeed, for most purposes it still is. As the world became more complex, as quantitative techniques developed, and as the information needs of science, government, and industry grew, new computing tools came along. The development of these tools, from the ancient abacus and the first mechanical calculators and slide rules in the early seventeenth century to the now-ubiquitous electronic calculator, is a fascinating story of human ambition and ingenuity. From our perspective, all of these tools are improvements over the brain in one way or another. The slide rule is quite a bit faster, though not always more accurate. Mechanical and electro-mechanical calculators are a little faster, more accurate, and have a bit more capacity. Electronic calculators are the same, but can do more (e.g. statistical and trigonometric functions).

It may surprise you to realize that the little electronic calculator you use to do your statistics homework or balance your checkbook is only a modest improvement over the brain. After all, it always produces the right answer, instantly – as soon as you press the = key, there it is. Ah – but what was your little calculator doing before you pressed the = key? It was waiting for you to key in all the numbers you wanted to add. In short, the calculator is a great tool, but as long as it depends on your hand to give it data it's not going to be much faster than your brain.

graphical data
storage tools

This brings us to the second kind of tool we need for data analysis: a tool for storing data. For most of our history, we have stored data graphically – by writing them down. Many natural materials have been used as data storage media: stone, clay, wax, wood, cloth, papyrus, skin, and paper. Each has its own virtues and drawbacks, but all graphical data storage media have the same limitation that we just discovered: they depend on a human eye/brain/hand system to transfer data between the storage medium and the computing tool. You have to read numbers from your checkbook, key them into your calculator, compute, and then read the result from the calculator and write it down in your checkbook. The development of faster computing tools is only half of the story. The other half is the development of data storage media that could be combined with a computing tool in a way that takes the human out of the loop.

non-graphical data
storage tools

In the past two centuries human ingenuity has produced an amazing collection of non-graphical data storage media: punch cards, paper tape, magnetic tape, magnetic disks, optical disks, holograms, and many more. Some are faster, more compact, and more reliable than others, but what all have in common is that they store data not as graphical symbols but as codes. For example, the IBM card used holes in different positions to represent different digits and letters. Floppy disks use a different (binary) code and magnetic charges instead of holes, but they do exactly the same thing. Along with the non-graphical media came gadgets – card readers, tape drives, disk drives, and the like – that could transfer data directly from storage medium to computing tool and from computing tool to storage medium. Even the slowest of these data-transfer gadgets is many times faster than the eye/brain/hand; as a result the computing tool spends less time waiting for data, and we start to see some real action.

programmability

Finally, let's return to the brain's great asset as a computing tool: its flexibility. I have in front of me a standard electronic calculator. It can add, subtract, multiply and divide. It can take percentages and square roots. It can do all this with real numbers of up to eight digits, flawlessly and instantly. But that's it. As long as my task is within these boundaries I'm ok, but if I need logarithms or cosines or need to work with huge or tiny numbers I have two choices. One is to use a bigger, fancier calculator. The other, more general solution is to use a more flexible computing tool: one that can be programmed. To program something – an alarm clock, a VCR, a computer – is to specify which of its elementary functions – ring a bell, start the tape, add two numbers – to carry out and in what order. As a programmer I am still limited to a machine's elementary functions, so I can't program my alarm clock to do calculations or my word processor to make toast. Nevertheless, if the elementary functions are elementary enough, programmability makes a machine extremely powerful and flexible.

The combination of a fast, accurate, programmable computing tool, non-graphical data storage medium, and no-hands data-transfer gadget that is most familiar to most of us is known as a computer. It's true that even very slow computers are faster than brains, which means that they enable us to get more work done in a given amount of time, but the greater significance of the computer is that by virtue of its speed, its direct access to data, and its programmability it enables us to do kinds of work that would otherwise be impossibly time consuming or just impossible. Some examples of these new kinds of work are obvious: computers let us write, communicate, play games, and do business in ways that would otherwise be impossible. Other examples are less obvious but very important for us. Data analysis involves manipulating data – moving, transforming, rearranging, combining – and doing statistical calculations. The computer really shines in both kinds of tasks, allowing us to work with colossal piles of data and to perform statistical calculations that would for all practical purposes be impossible to do by hand.

2.2   Software

The third and final tool that we need for data analysis, and the one that this book is most concerned with, is the program, or software (computing tools and data storage media are hardware), that tells the computer what to do, when and how to do it, what data to use, where to find the data, how to present the results, and so forth. The typical computer is equipped with many kinds of software, but the only kind that concerns us is statistical software.

> *Software tools let us communicate with computing and data storage tools.*

There are probably hundreds of statistical software packages out there, and the differences among them are at first bewildering. Some are easy for almost anyone to use, while others give even data professionals headaches and short tempers. Some are free, while others are obscenely expensive. Some fit on a floppy disk, while others consume vast amounts of disk space and memory. Some are fairly limited, while others can do nearly anything with nearly unlimited amounts of data. Under the skin, however, there are some things all of them have in common. Let us consider the functional parts of a statistics program.

Input processes. The first step in any analysis is getting data into the computer (see 3.7). Data may be keyed in from the keyboard, read from various kinds of files, or pasted directly from another application. Some programs are more flexible and versatile than others.

> *the parts of statistical software*

Data editor. Most programs have a spreadsheet-style data editor. In general, you do things to data in the data editor and you do things *with* data outside of it, but there is a good deal of variation. This book is more concerned with doing things to data, or *data manipulation*, and we will spend a good deal of time in data editors.

User interface. This is the part of the software through which you interact with the various tools. There are two kinds of interface. A *command-driven* interface requires us to issue commands that the system can execute. An example that everyone is familiar with is the user interface of the HAL9000, the (fictional) computer in the movie *2001*. The astronauts interact with the computer by speaking commands, e.g. "Open the pod bay doors, HAL." HAL "understands" the command because it is programmed to process English syntax. Syntax is the set of rules in a language that specify how sentences in that language can (and cannot) be structured. In English we can say

> *If all else fails, read the manual.*

or

> *Read the manual if all else fails.*

or several other variations, but we can't say

> *If fails manual read the all else.*

That's syntax. Statistical software is not as sophisticated as HAL, but it can process the syntax of a specialized command language. If the software wants us to ask for the mean of variable X by typing

```
compute mean X
```

then it will not accept

```
compute X mean.
```

Command-driven software has become unpopular because you have to remember or look up the commands and their syntax and because you have to do a lot of typing. The alternative is menu-driven software, in which instead of typing commands you choose what you want to do from a list (menu) of choices, usually by clicking a mouse. In the last example we would have to choose *mean* from a list of statistics that are available, and then we would choose *X* from a list of the variables in our data set. For example, if you wanted to run a t-test comparing mean yield per acre of two varieties of soybeans you would go through a series of menus something like this (in each menu our choice is highlighted):

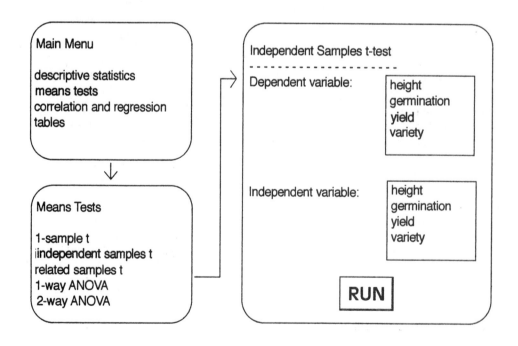

The three menus are the equivalent of the pseudocode command

```
> compute t(unpaired) yield, groups are variety=1,2
```

Both types of software have advantages and disadvantages. Command-driven software requires memory (human) and typing, whereas menu-driven software shows us what our choices are at any given point. On the other hand, there are often many menus to go through before the program has all the information it needs to do what you want it to do, and this can be just as tedious as typing commands, if not more so. Although the two interfaces may look and feel very different, a t-test is a t-test, and whether you use commands or menus you must tell the program what it needs to know. We will use commands because they are easier to put in a book, but you should bear in mind that if we were using menus we would have to provide the computer with the same information.

In addition to the command system, the user interface usually includes a help system. Some help systems are quite good, but most are not especially helpful. None is a substitute for a good manual. Finally, most programs also provide ways to control the software, from the shading of a bar graph or the size of a plotting symbol to the number of decimal places to display to the confidence level we want the program to use if we don't tell it otherwise.

Data manipulation tools. These are the tools that this book is about; there are tools that restructure data sets (ch. 4), tools that create new variables (ch. 6), tools that combine data sets (ch. 7), tools that aggregate data (ch. 10), and others.

Statistical computation tools. These are the tools that compute the various descriptive and inferential statistics. Different packages use different computational methods, which sometimes yield slightly different results from a given set of data. These differences are of interest to mathematical statisticians and programmers, but for most users and most purposes the differences are trivial and can be ignored. It matters far more what statistic you choose to compute than what program you use to compute it.

Graphing tools. Most software will do at least some basic graphing, and some packages have virtually unlimited graphing capability. Different programs have very different approaches to graphing, and the differences in structure and terminology can be confusing. Because there is usually no single correct way to graph a set of data, graphing tools require us to be very specific about what we want.

Output operations. There are two kinds of output (results – i.e. the things you create using the tools – and data) and there are three ways to output them (display, print, file). You can print a graph, save data in a file, or display a table on the screen. One kind of output deserves special mention: the *log file*. In a typical session at the computer, we are likely to issue many commands and generate a considerable amount of potential output. Rather than printing everything we do, which is wasteful and slow, we can create a log file, a continuous record of every command and every result. Later we can edit the log file to find stuff we want to print or to copy into something we're writing, etc. The log file solves the problem we run into when we generate a result that is bigger than the screen, or a number of related results that we need to look at together. Another advantage is that if we need to perform the same analysis with another data set – a very common situation – the log file serves as a script. A variant of the log file is the *command file*, which lists only the commands we've issued in a given analysis. Repeating that analysis is now even easier, because the command file amounts to a program; it is analogous to a macro in a word processor.

The diagram below summarizes the functional anatomy of a statistical program.

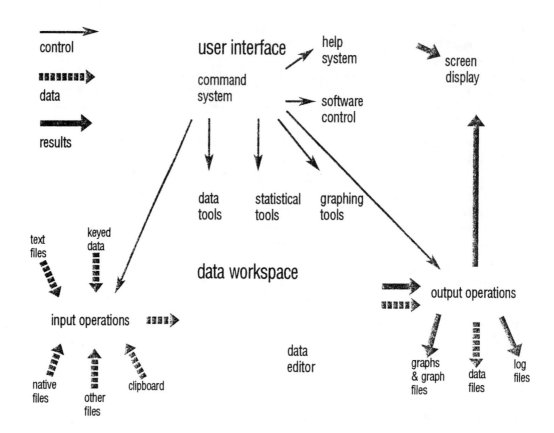

2.3   What doesn't statistical software do?

No software, no matter how exhaustive its collection of statistics, how splendid its graphs, or how powerful its data handling procedures, can (or should) tell us how to analyze our data, check the appropriateness of what we're doing with our data, or interpret our results. Computers and their software are tools and nothing more. As with any other tool you, the user, are responsible for doing the right thing.

Data in the computer

Chapter Outline

1. A data file is set up like a spreadsheet.
2. Computers treat integers and real numbers differently.
3. Statistical software can't do much with string variables.
4. When possible, string variables should be encoded as numeric variables.
5. A coded variable should always have its (numeric) values labeled with the strings they encode.
6. Missing values must be represented explicitly.
7. There are many ways to get data into the computer.
8. A code book or data dictionary lists all the variables in a data set as well as their codes and labels.

THE FIRST STEP in data analysis is getting the data into the computer. To do this successfully it helps to think about data the way the computer does. In this chapter we will consider some of the differences between the way we handle numbers and letters and the way computers do, and then discuss various ways of creating a data file.

3.1 Data files

From our point of view a set of data consists of *cases* (or *records*) and *variables*. (As we'll see later, the computer's point of view is different.) If we ask each of four people how many pets and how many children they have, then we have four cases (the people) and two variables (number of pets, number of children), and we would most likely record our data like this:

```
person#    #pets    #children
1          12       3
2          1        2
3          0        4
4          5        0
```

When we put these data into a computer, it seems quite natural to arrange our data in the form of a spreadsheet:

*data in a spread-
sheet-style data
editor*

	# pets	# children			
1	12	3			
2	1	2			
3	0	4			
4	5	0			
5					
6					

Each row is a case, and each column is a variable. Case 1, whoever s/he may be, has twelve pets and three kids; case 2 has one pet and two kids; and so on. The empty rows and columns reflect the fact that in principle a spreadsheet goes on indefinitely in both dimensions; we can (and often do) add more cases or more variables. The only limit to such expansion, when there is one, is the amount of memory and/or disk space in a computer. (Paper is also a limited resource, and from here on I will omit the extra space.) Each box in the spreadsheet is called a *cell*, and each cell that isn't empty contains a value. It is perhaps unfortunate that *variable* and *value* both begin with *v*, for a large proportion of the trouble that beginning data analysts experience comes from confusing the two. A variable is a measure or classification that varies, or differs, from case to case. A value, on the other hand, belongs to a single case. In the example, the number of pets varies from case to case; #pets is a variable. Case 3 has zero pets; zero is the value of the variable #pets for case 3.

*variable names
and variable labels*

What about the gray parts? The top row is not a case; it holds the names of the variables. A *variable name* is what we use to tell the computer which variable we want it to do something with. A variable must have a name, and if we don't give it one the software will, e.g. var1. If we want to know the mean number of pets we say

```
> compute mean of #pets
```

and we get

```
        mean    n
#pets    4.5    4
```

This is fine, so long as the person looking at this output knows exactly what #pets is. Given that others often look at our output, and that we often forget things, it is good practice to give #pets a *variable label*. This may sound like a label that varies, but in fact it's a label that describes a variable. If we label #pets

```
> assign var #pets label = 'no. of pets in household'
```

then when we ask for the mean of #pets

```
> compute mean of #pets
```

we get

```
                            mean    n
no. of pets in household     4.5    4
```

Why go to all this trouble? Why not use longer variable names? There's a good reason. A variable name is used a lot. It has to appear in menus and we have to type it. It needs to be short, and in fact most software severely limits the length of variable names. On the other hand, we want a label to be clear and complete, so it has a much more liberal length limit.

Back to our spreadsheet. The other gray area, the first column, is not a variable; it holds the row numbers. Notice I didn't say case numbers. If we sort the data in ascending order of number of pets

case numbers and row numbers

```
> sort on #pets, ascending
```

we will get this:

	# pets	# children			
1	0	4			
2	1	2			
3	5	0			
4	12	3			

The row numbers are the same, but the values in a given row have changed. Is case 1 the values that are now in row 1, or is it the values that were originally in the first row and are now in row 3? It's all the same to the computer, so if it matters to us we need explicitly to include a case number variable in the data set:

	case_id	# pets	# children		
1	1	12	3		
2	2	1	2		
3	3	0	4		
4	4	5	0		

Now when we sort the data we don't lose track of which case is which:

	case_id	# pets	# children		
1	3	0	4		
2	2	1	2		
3	4	5	0		
4	1	12	3		

How many variables are there in this data set now? The computer would say three, because there are three columns in the spreadsheet, but we would say two, because case_id is not a measurement or a classification; it is an identifier, and although the computer wouldn't know the difference it would be meaningless to use case_id in any calculations.

It is generally good practice to assign an identification number to every case you collect data from, whether your cases are people, rats, baseball teams, or buildings. If you give people questionnaires to fill out, you should number them after they have all been returned (so you can't know which number goes with which person) and then enter the number along with the data. If you're working with rats you should number the rats' cages, and record each rat's cage number along with whatever data you're collecting from the animal. Having case identification numbers can be very useful in correcting errors in the data, as we will see in Chapter 4. You may never need them, but if you do need them and don't have them you will kick yourself.

3.2   Data storage types

Characters are represented as symbols.

Computers are binary creatures. This means that everything in a computer – an instruction, a number, a color, a word, a sound – is represented by one or more binary digits, otherwise known as bits. A bit can have one of two values: 0 and 1. If we need to represent something that has only two possible values, then one bit is enough, but if there are more than two possible values we need more bits. For example, there are 128 basic characters that a computer can display, and to assign a unique set of bits to each one we need seven bits. For most purposes computers use eight bits, or one byte, per character. To store the word "digital" would require seven bytes of memory or disk space.

Numbers are represented as quantities.

What about numbers? You might be tempted to assume that if a word requires one byte per character, a number would need one byte per digit. This can be done, and sometimes is[1], but in fact we need only one byte to represent the numbers 0 to 255, because eight bits have 256 possible values. There are two important points here. The first is that characters, and everything made from them, are stored as symbols, while numbers are stored as quantities. Each bit in a byte represents a power of two:

$2^7=128$	$2^6=64$	$2^5=32$	$2^4=16$	$2^3=8$	$2^2=4$	$2^1=2$	$2^0=1$
1	1	0	1	0	1	1	0

For example, the number 214 would be stored in the byte 11010110. Reading this byte from right to left, we get

$$
\begin{array}{rcr}
0 \times 1 & = & 0 \\
1 \times 2 & = & 2 \\
1 \times 4 & = & 4 \\
0 \times 8 & = & 0 \\
1 \times 16 & = & 16 \\
0 \times 32 & = & 0 \\
1 \times 64 & = & 64 \\
1 \times 128 & = & 128 \\
\hline
 & & 214
\end{array}
$$

On the other hand, if we include 214 in text – e.g. "There are 214 cows on this farm" – then it will be treated as three symbols, 2, 1, 4, and would be stored in the bytes 00110010 00110001 00110100. If we decode these bytes as numbers as we did in the previous example, we get 50, 49, 52 respectively, indicating the 50th, 49th, and 52nd characters in the computer's

---

[1] Primarily in accounting, where rounding errors are unacceptable (see below).

character set, which happen to be 2, 1, and 4.

The second point is that everything takes up space, in memory and on disk. Not too long ago these were scarce resources. Today they are less scarce, but still finite, and in any case it is good practice to use no more space, particularly in memory, than you need. Encoding 214 as the binary number 11010110 takes less space than encoding it as the characters 2,1,4, but there are two limitations to this kind of binary encoding. First, very big numbers use up a lot of bits: a number 30 decimal digits long would take up 100 bits. Second, we are limited to integers (whole numbers). Both problems can be solved by using a representation based on scientific notation. The idea is simple: any real number can be expressed as a positive or negative power of ten multiplied by a positive or negative number between zero and ten. Here are some examples:

700,000,000,000	=	7×10^{11}
7300,000,000,000	=	7.3×10^{11}
703,000,000,000	=	7.03×10^{11}
-700,000,000,000	=	-7×10^{11}
0.00000482	=	4.82×10^{-6}
-0.00000482	=	-4.82×10^{-6}

> *Large, small, and non-integer numbers need a different kind of representation.*

Scientific notation not only produces a compact representation of very big and very small numbers, but also makes arithmetic much easier (and faster) for the computer. However, there is a compromise between compactness and precision:

703,972,245,086	=	$7.03972245086 \times 10^{11}$

No savings here; to make this number compact we have to sacrifice some precision, for example by rounding to the nearest 1,000,000:

703,972,245,086	=	7.03972×10^{11}

This is probably ok if you're calculating intergalactic distances, but the IRS may object. The details of *floating-point* (non-integer) representation don't concern us here. What matters to us is that the computer's way of storing floating-point numbers can lead to a loss of precision in computations with very big and very small numbers. How very is very? It depends on the number of *significant digits* available for the first part of the expression; the more digits you can represent, the less rounding you have to do.

To summarize, the computer has three distinct kinds of representation: symbolic, integer, and floating-point. Every value of a given variable is represented in the same way, using the same number of bytes. Ideally, we want this number to be just enough to handle the largest value that variable can take on, but we don't always know what that maximum value is. Most statistical software deals with this problem in fairly intelligent ways, always striving to err on the side of too many bits, because this only wastes space while too few can cause computational errors. In general, the strategy is to allocate enough bytes to handle very large numbers, and to increase this allocation if a larger number is encountered.

3.3   Strings

The value of a variable may be a number (either integer or floating-point), or it may be one or more characters, in which case we call it a *string* variable. In our pets-and-kids data set we could include the name of each of our respondents:

> *A series of characters is a string.*

	case_id	name	# pets	# children	
1	1	Mary Jane	12	3	
2	2	Ed	1	2	
3	3	Alice	0	4	
4	4	Sviatoslav	5	0	

String variables can be used to sort data, and they can be included in certain kinds of output. For instance, I use statistical software in lieu of a grade book. I make a separate file for each class, and record each student's name and scores on quizzes:

	name	quiz1	quiz2	quiz3		
1	Nora	92	85	84		
2	Cora	74	81	72		
3	Dora	95	99	98		
4	Flora	81	85	83		

Then I use the software to compute each student's average (a floating-point variable) and assign a letter grade (another string variable):

	name	quiz1	quiz2	quiz3	average	grade
1	Nora	92	85	84	87.0	B
2	Cora	74	81	72	75.7	C
3	Dora	97	100	98	98.3	A+
4	Flora	81	84	83	82.7	B-

Finally, I can produce an alphabetic grade list:

```
> sort on name, ascending
> list name, grade

  Cora    C
  Dora    A+
  Flora   B-
  Nora    B
```

3.4   Encoding strings

In the grade book example, the value of name is probably unique in most cases; we don't necessarily expect a given value (a name) to occur more than once. In contrast, suppose I add another string variable in which I record each student's major:

	name	major	quiz1	quiz2	quiz3	
1	Nora	English	92	85	84	
2	Cora	philosophy	74	81	72	
3	Dora	philosophy	95	99	98	
4	Flora	English	81	85	83	

The value of major is not necessarily unique; we do expect a given value (a major) to occur more than once. If I want to know how students in each major are doing in my course, I could use this new variable to break down the data by major, giving me the mean score for English majors on each of the three quizzes, and likewise for philosophy majors (and any other majors represented in the class). The only problem is

```
> compute mean of quiz1, quiz2, quiz3, by major
```

```
***error***
```

it won't work. The software can't do much with strings, and one of the things it can't do is to use a string variable as a grouping variable, i.e. to break the data into groups. Fortunately there is a simple solution: we can *encode* the string variable. Instead of entering Nora's major as "english" I should enter it as "1," and instead of entering Cora's major as "philosophy" I should enter it as "2."

Strings are more useful when they are encoded.

	name	major	quiz1	quiz2	quiz3	
1	Nora	1	92	85	84	
2	Cora	2	74	81	72	
3	Dora	2	95	99	98	
4	Flora	1	81	85	83	

The 1s and 2s are codes; 1 stands for English and 2 stands for philosophy. Now major is a numeric variable, and the command should work:

```
> compute mean of quiz1, quiz2, quiz3, by major

major    quiz1   quiz2   quiz3

1        86.5    85.0    83.5
2        84.5    90.0    85.0
```

3.5 Value labels

This is progress, but we've lost something, too. To read the output above I have to refer to the paper where I wrote down

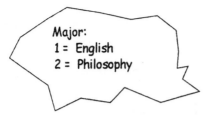

This is a nuisance, and if I lose the paper I'm sunk. The solution is to label the values.

value	label
1	English
2	Philosophy

Encoded strings should have labeled values.

The values remain numbers, so the computer can work with them, and the values have string labels, so the output will be self-explanatory:

```
major        quiz1   quiz2   quiz3

English       86.5    85.0    83.5
Philosophy    84.5    90.0    85.0
```

How is this different from a string variable? If we use a string variable, every English major will have the string "English" as the value of major; "English" will appear as many times as there are English majors. Using a labeled numeric variable, on the other hand, every English major will have the number 1 as the value of major. The string "English" will not appear at all in the data set, but in any output (a list, a table, etc.) whenever the value of major is 1 we will see instead "English."

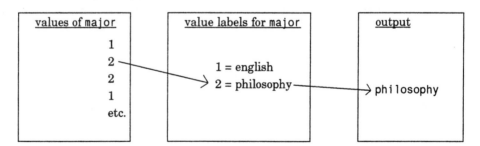

3.6   Missing values

So far we have been assuming that we live in a perfect data world, and that we have a value for every variable for every case. In the real world, of course, data sets often have a few empty cells. People leave items blank on questionnaires, make illegible responses, check two options on "check one of the following" items, write down their age instead of their weight, and so on. When there is no response or the response is ambiguous or impossible, there is nothing to enter. What should you do? Leave it blank? Let's try it:

	case_id	name	# pets	# children	
1	1	Mary Jane	12	3	
2	2	Ed		2	
3	3	Alice	0	4	
4	4	Sviatoslav	5	0	

Perhaps Ed has answered the question "How many pets do you have?" by writing "yes," or perhaps he has not answered it. In either case we have nothing to enter, so we leave that cell empty. This seems perfectly reasonable, and, on paper, it is. The problem is that computers don't use paper; they use digital representations of information. What is the digital representation of a blank?

This is not as simple a question as it sounds. The answer emphasizes the difference that we discussed earlier between symbolic and numeric representations. String and character variables are symbolic, and it is no problem to create a special symbol, the *null character*, to designate nothing, no value, blank. The null is represented by the byte 00000000. When the computer encounters a null in the context of a string variable, the computer understands this to mean "there's nothing here."

How we represent nothing depends on what isn't there.

However, this strategy won't work for a numeric variable, because the pattern of bits is interpreted not as a symbol but as a number, so the computer understands 00000000 to mean *zero*. The problem is that nothing is not a number (it's not the same as zero, as we've just seen), and therefore can't be represented by a numeric variable.

The solution is to designate a special number to represent missing numeric values. For example, if we use a byte to represent the integers -127 through +126, there is one more number (+127) that we can treat as a missing value. Different statistics packages have different ways of representing missing values, but the basic strategy is the same: reserve a value outside of the range of values that a variable can take on, and treat that extreme value as missing. If we ask for the mean number of pets

```
> compute mean of #pets
```

the computer will (a) add all the non-missing values of #pets, (b) count all the non-missing values of #pets, and (c) divide the sum by the count to find the mean. Ed has been left out of this computation. On the other hand, if we ask for a list of people and their numbers of pets in ascending order of #pets

```
> sort on #pets, ascending
> list name, #pets
```

Alice   0
Sviatoslav   5
Mary Jane   12
Ed   .

the computer includes Ed (the dot indicates a missing value). It would have been inappropriate to include Ed's missing value in the mean calculation, but there is no harm in sorting missing values – indeed, we will see that it is sometimes very useful. Ed came out last in this sort because his missing value is represented by a large number; if instead it were represented by a very small number he would be listed first.

The good news about missing values is that the software generally takes care of everything for you. You don't have to choose a value to represent missing (though you can if necessary) and you don't have to tell the computer how to handle missing values. However, you do need to pay attention to what your software does with missing values in order to use it properly and understand your results. The difference between including and excluding missing values can be quite important, as we will see.

<table>
<tr><td>

Don't ignore missing values.
</td><td>

Scene: A busy urban street corner. Earnest-looking young people with clipboards attempt to engage passers by in conversation. One student stops an elderly woman.
</td></tr>
</table>

Student:	Excuse me, ma'am, I'm conducting a survey for my History of Drug Abuse course, and I'd like to ask you a few questions.
Woman:	(*smugly*) Well! I certainly don't use drugs, but go ahead, ask your questions.
Student:	Thank you. First of all, how old are you?
Woman:	Too old to lie about it. I'm 86.
Student:	Have you ever smoked marijuana?
Woman:	(*shocked*) Why, no! I've never used any...
Student:	(*cuts her off*) Ever used cocaine?
Woman:	(*aghast*) Of course not! I told you, I've...
Student:	Sorry, I have to ask. Do you drink coffee?
Woman:	(*recovering*) Oh, yes. Two cups every morning. Helps the digestion, you know.
Student:	Do you smoke?
Woman:	Mm-hm. Doctor says it's bad for me, but... (*fumbles in her purse*)
Student:	Last question: how much do you drink?
Woman:	(*catching on*) None of your business, young lady! (*walks away fuming*)

What should the student do when she enters the data from this interview? Saying that information about the respondent's drinking is missing doesn't capture the flavor of the exchange: the information was withheld. Sometimes missing is missing, and it doesn't matter why, but sometimes it is useful to distinguish among the different reasons for values being missing. Here's a tentative classification:

1) Accidentally missing:
- data loss due to equipment malfunction
- data loss due to acts of God, dogs, or children
- researcher error (forgetting to ask a question, etc.)
- respondent oversight (neglecting a questionnaire item, etc.)

2) Unusable:
- illegible response
- too many responses ("What's your favorite color?" "Blue and red.")
- impossible response ("What's your favorite color?" "Moby Dick.")

3) Intentionally missing:
- respondent deliberately skipped a questionnaire item
- respondent explicitly declined to answer

4) Other:
- experimental subject did not respond within time limit
- subject in longitudinal study died, moved, dropped out, etc

Whether you should make any distinctions, and if so what kind, is between you and your research. I only want to raise the issue and to give you a sense of what can be done. Our drug-abuse researcher might enter her data using the following encoding scheme for item 6 ("How much do you drink?"):

code	label
1	none
2	1 glass/day or less
3	2 glasses/day
4	3 glasses/day
5	more than 3 glasses/day
9	no response

If a response to this question was accidentally lost or destroyed it would be entered as missing, like Ed's pets. This is called a *system missing value*, because it is represented by a value designated by the system (specifically, the software). If, on the other hand, there is no response because the respondent explicitly declined to answer, it would be entered as a 9. This is called a *user missing value*, because it is a value designated by the user. In doing this we turn the absence of a piece of information into a piece of information in its own right.

Another way to appreciate the difference between system missing and user missing values is to look at some output. Suppose our researcher interviewed 100 people. After entering all the data using the encoding scheme above, she asks for a tabulation of responses to the drinking question:

```
> tabulate row=item6

How much do you drink?     freq.   %

none                       12      12.00
1 glass/day or less        19      19.00
2 glasses/day              23      23.00
3 glasses/day              15      15.00
more than 3 glasses/day    13      13.00
no response                18      18.00
total                      100     100.00
```

Alternatively, suppose she treats the non-responses as system missing. Now her output will look like this:

```
How much do you drink?     freq.   %

none                       12      14.63
1 glass/day or less        19      23.17
2 glasses/day              23      28.05
3 glasses/day              15      18.29
more than 3 glasses/day    13      15.85
total                      82      100.00
```

The 18 respondents who didn't answer this question are not counted, and as a result the percentages must be read with care. In the first table the percentage for the response "none" is 12.00, meaning that 12% *of the people interviewed* said they do not drink at all. In the second table this percentage changes to 14.63, meaning that 14.63% *of those who answered the question* said they do not drink at all. Both figures are meaningful and potentially significant, but it is very important to keep them straight, especially when non-responders constitute a substantial proportion of the sample.

3.7   Getting data into the computer

By now you have a pretty good idea of how data should be arranged in the computer, but how do you get them in there in the first place? There are four ways to do this, ranging from the trivially simple to the monumentally tedious. Unfortunately, you don't usually have much choice in the matter.

data files

Native files. Most statistical software saves data using a file format that is unique to that software. This means the file can be used only by that software. If someone gives you some data in your software's file format, or if you're using data you saved on a previous occasion, you're in luck. Open the file and get to work.

Text files. A text file is limited, roughly, to the characters that appear on a keyboard. It has no pictures, graphics, web links, or formatting codes, so it can be read by virtually anything. Although a text file isn't the most convenient way of getting data into your program, it is often the only way. For example, most of my experiments are run by a computer. The machine presents stimuli to subjects, collects their responses, and saves them in a text file. Then I read the text file into my statistical software, fix it up a bit, and save it as a native file. From then on, when I work with these data I can use the native file. The main difference is that when you use a text file you have to tell your software exactly what it's going to find in the file, whereas a native file takes care of this for you.

The potential difficulty in using text files comes from the fact there are two basic ways, and many variants of each, to format a text file. Both *free format* and *fixed format* are solutions to the same problem: How do we tell the computer where each value begins and ends? Free format files require us to tell the computer what separates, or delimits, the values of each case. Here are some examples:

text file formats

```
1) Tab-delimited:      1    "Mary Jane"    12    3
                       2    "Ed"            .    2
                       3    "Alice"         0    4
                       4    "Sviatoslav"    5    0

2) Space-delimited:    1 "Mary Jane" 12 3
                       2 "Ed" . 2
                       3 "Alice" 0 4
                       4 "Sviatoslav" 5 0

3) Comma-delimited:    1,Mary Jane,12,3
                       2,Ed,.,2
                       3,Alice,0,4
                       4,Sviatoslav,5,0
```

The computer treats a tab, a space, or a comma as the end of a value. To read this file we would say

```
> read free file petsandkids.txt, variables are case_id,
name(string), pets, kids
```

This tells the program that in each row, the first value it reads is case_id, the second is name, and so on. Quotation marks around strings are sometimes optional, unless the string contains the character that is being used as the delimiter, as "Mary Jane" does in the space-delimited file. We are using a period (.) to represent a missing value, but this is not a universal practice. Notice that we had to explicitly identify name as a string variable but we didn't have to identify the others as numeric variables. Statistics being a largely numerical sort of enterprise, it is reasonable to let the computer assume that a variable is numeric unless we tell it otherwise. Most software makes many such assumptions; we call these *defaults* or *default values*.

Fixed format files require us to tell the computer where each value begins and ends rather than what separates them. A computer treats a text file like a piece of graph paper, with rows and columns defining discrete cells. Each cell contains exactly one character, so it is possible to specify which column a value begins in and which column it ends in. Here is an example:

```
4) Fixed-format:    1Mary Jane   123
                    2Ed           .2
                    3Alice        04
                    4Sviatoslav   50
```

Notice that no quotation marks are needed, regardless of what's in the string. To read this file we would say

```
>read fixed file petsandkids.txt, variables are case_id(1),
name(string)(2), pets(12), kids(13)
```

This tells the program that in each row, the value of case_id begins in column 1, name begins in column 2, and so on.

For data that are entirely or mostly numeric, fixed format files have the advantage of being smaller than free format files. For a very large data set this advantage can be substantial, which makes fixed format the best choice if you need to cram a lot of stuff into limited disk space or if you might need to send the file by modem.

Non-native files. What if you have a file that was created by a different program? Unless that program is obscure, the chances are good that you can find *data conversion* or *data translation* software. If you can't, but you have access to the other program, you can open the file, save it in ASCII (plain text) format, then read the ASCII file into your program as described above.

From scratch. Entering data from scratch goes pretty quickly if there aren't more than, say, a couple of hundred cases and a dozen or so variables, but it can be very easy to collect a lot more data than this, and if you have to enter them all by hand you are in for quite a bit of painstaking typing. Let me put it more strongly: if at all possible, avoid designing your research in a way that requires you to enter a lot of data by hand. On the other hand, if you're collecting a small number of data, don't go to great lengths to avoid typing. There are three approaches to entering data.

entering data by hand

Make a text file. This is a low-tech approach that has the advantage of producing a file that you can use with any software. To make a text file, choose a file format (see above) and use either a *text editor* or a word processor to do the typing. A text editor is a small, simple, fast relative of the word processor that creates text files and is ideal for this job. If you use a word processor, your job will be easier if you use a non-proportional type face, but in either case you must save your work as a text file rather than as a word processor file.

Use the data editor. Most statistical software has a built-in spreadsheet-style data editor. Each has its own characteristics, but all use the same basic arrangement: each column is a variable, and each row is a case. Once you've entered the data this way you can save them in the program's native format for future use.

Set up a database. If you have a lot of data, or you have a big grant, or you enjoy database programming, this is the way to go. A database program allows you to design a *data entry screen*, which interactively prompts you for each variable, checks for values that are illegal, impossible, too long, etc., and fills in defaults. Your typing goes faster and you'll make fewer errors, but the up-front costs in programming time may be considerable.

3.8   Code books and data dictionaries

You are on an archaeological dig at the recently discovered site of Um, the ancient capital of the Num civilization. Carefully sifting through the sand, you imagine the thrill of being the first to find some written record of Num culture. You start to remind yourself that your team has been digging and sifting for six months and has found nothing but broken clay vessels smelling faintly of beer, when you notice something a little different sticking out of the sand. Trembling with anticipation, you pick up what appears to be a clay tablet. Here's what it says:

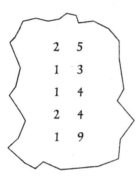

Eureka! The ancient and mysterious Num were not only the earliest known alcoholics, but appear to have been the earliest statisticians as well. You drop your shovel and rush to your tent, turn on your laptop and... what? What are these numbers? What can you learn from them?

Sadly, the answer is: probably nothing. Unless... unless... Unless! Back at the site you dig a little farther. The secrets of the Num will remain locked in the sands unless you can find the key. What's that sticking out there? It looks like the same clay as the tablet was made from; in fact it looks like

Beer Survey
Item 1: Do you prefer Zum or Zum Lite?
     1 Zum
     2 Zum Lite
     9 no response
Item 2: How many clay vessels do you drink in a day?
     1 none
     2 1 to 3
     3 4 to 6
     4 6 to 9
     5 10 or more
     9 no response

You have found the *code book*, which allows you to make sense of the data tablet. A code book lists the variables in a data set, explaining what you need to know about each one, namely:

a) What does this variable measure?
b) What unit of measurement does this variable use?

It is not enough to know what a variable measures. Our drug abuse researcher's first question ("How old are you?") will presumably become a variable that measures age. But how? Depending on whether we are working with fruit flies, infants, children, or adults we can use days, weeks, months, or years; depending on what we want to do with the age variable we can measure age quantitatively (e.g. 48 years old) or categorically (e.g. 45-50 years old). A code book is the place to record, for future archaeologists' and your own use, both what and how a variable measures.

Here is what the code book for the drug abuse interview might look like:

Item:	1
Question:	How old are you?
Variable:	age
Values:	positive integers representing age in years
Item	2
Question:	Have you ever smoked marijuana?
Variable:	smokepot
Values:	*code* *label*
	0 no
	1 yes
	9 no response

a sample
code book

Item	3
Question:	Have you ever used cocaine?
Variable:	usecoke
Values:	*code* *label*
	0 no
	1 yes
	9 no response

Item	4
Question:	Do you drink coffee?
Variable:	drcoffee
Values:	*code* *label*
	0 no
	1 yes
	9 no response

Item	5
Question:	Do you smoke?
Variable:	smoke
Values:	*code* *label*
	0 no
	1 yes
	9 no response

Item:	6
Question:	How much do you drink?
Variable:	amtdrink
Responses:	*code* *label*
	0 none
	1 1 glass/day or less
	2 2 glasses/day
	3 3 glasses/day
	4 more than 3 glasses/day
	9 no response

Often it is possible to build the code book into a questionnaire:

1. What is your age in years? _____
2. Have you ever smoked marijuana?   (0)_____ no
.   (1)_____ yes
.   (9)_____ I prefer not to answer
.

6. How much do you drink?   (0)_____ none
                                                                     (1)_____ 1 glass/day or less
                                                                     (2)_____ 2 glasses/day
                                                                     (3)_____ 3 glasses/day
                                                                     (4)_____ more than 3 glasses/day
                                                                     (9)_____ I prefer not to answer

Constructing a questionnaire this way makes things easier for the person doing the data entry and cuts down on errors. Whether you're running a laboratory experiment, making field observations, interviewing people door-to-door, or doing a questionnaire study, make the code book before you collect any data. A little thought about what you're going to wind up with and how you're going to get it into the computer can prevent some nasty surprises down the road.

A relative of the code book is the *data dictionary*, which is essentially a machine-readable code book. A data dictionary documents your data and simplifies the process of reading them into the machine. A dictionary for the drug abuse data might look like this (anything in [brackets] is a comment and is ignored by the machine):

```
*dictionary = drugdata
     format=free
     var age=integer               [age in years; 0=no response]
     var smokepot=integer          [ever smoke pot?]
     label smokepot values=0/no 1/yes 9/no response
     var usecoke=integer           [ever use cocaine?]
     label usecoke values=0/no 1/yes 9/no response
     var drcoffee=integer          [drink coffee?]
     label drcoffee=0/no 1/yes 9/no response
     var smoke=integer             [smoke?]
     label smoke values=0/no 1/yes 9/no response
     var amtdrink=integer          [how much do you drink?]
     label amtdrink values=0/none 1/1 glass/day or less 2/2
          glasses/day 3/3 glasses/day 4/more than 3 glasses/day 9/I
          prefer not to answer
end
86    0    0    1    1    9
32    1    1    1    0    0
48    1    0    1    1    4
59    0    0    1    1    3
etc...
```

To use these data, all we have to do is

```
> read file drugdata.txt
```

When the computer opens the file, it will find the dictionary, read it, and then read the data. Alternatively, the dictionary could be a separate file, in which case we'd say

```
> read file drugdata.txt, dictionary=drugdict.txt
```

Either way, using a dictionary with a text data file makes it as easy to use as a native file.

That's nice, but why didn't we make a native file instead? Often it makes little difference which way you go, but if you're going to have many files with the same variables, you'll save time and typing with the text-plus-dictionary approach. For example, if we do a weekly public opinion survey in which every week we call a different random sample of people and ask them the same set of questions, then we can put each week's data in a new text file, but we can keep using the same dictionary to read the data file.

3.9   Exercises

Put each of the data sets below into the computer, using your software's data editor. For each set, do the following:

      a. Enter the data.
      b. Label the variables.
      c. Encode and/or label values where appropriate.
      d. Make a code book.
      e. Save the data set as a native file.
      f. Load the native file to confirm that you have correctly saved the data.

1. Some notable bridges:

name	location	type	length(m)	crosses	built
Angostura	Venezuela	1	712	1	1967
Bayonne	USA	3	510	1	1931
Bosporus	Turkey	1	1074	3	1973
Brooklyn	USA	1	486	1	1883
Forth Railway	Scotland	2	521	2	1890
George Washington	USA	1	1067	1	1931
Golden Gate	USA	1	1280	2	1937
Howrah	India	2	457	1	1943
Humber	England	1	1410	1	1981
Kanmon Strait	Japan	1	712	3	1973
Laviolette	Canada	3	335	1	1967
Mackinac Straits	USA	1	1158	3	1957
Minato Ohashi	Japan	2	510	2	1974
New River Gorge	USA	3	518	1	1977
Patapsco River	USA	2	366	2	1976
Ponte 25 de Abril	Portugal	1	1013	1	1966
Quebec Railway	Canada	2	549	1	1917
Severn	England	1	988	1	1966
Sydney Harbor	Australia	3	509	2	1932
Verrazano	USA	1	1298	2	1964
Williamsburg	USA	1	488	1	1903

                                      1=suspension   1=river
                                        2=cantilever   2=harbor or bay
                                        3=steel arch   3=strait or channel

2. Suppose a telephone survey asks the following questions:

      1. What is your age?
      2. What is your sex?
      3. What is the last grade of school you completed?
      4. What is your marital status?
      5. How often do you read a newspaper?
      6. What kind of pickle do you prefer?

The survey is conducted in New York and Los Angeles. Here are some of the data:

resp#	location	age	sex	educ. level	mar. stat.	paper	pickle
1	NY	74	f	hs grad	widowed	daily	dill
2	NY	34	m	B.A.	divorced	rarely	half sour
3	LA	37	m	some coll.	no answer	usually	dill
4	NY	49	f	M.A.	married	daily	sour
5	LA	23	f	B.A.	single	rarely	none
6	LA	44	m	no answer	no answer	no answer	none
7	LA	29	m	B.A.	divorced	daily	dill
8	LA	61	f	hs grad	married	daily	half sour
9	NY	29	f	some coll.	single	usually	half sour
10	NY	58	m	Ph.D.	married	no answer	sour

. . .

Demonstration 1

Looking at Faces, Part I

RECENTLY ONE OF MY STUDENTS, Dennis Dickinson, did a study investigating the relation between perceived happiness and perceived attractiveness. Dennis wanted to know if faces that are perceived as happier are also perceived as more attractive, and vice versa. Using black-and-white yearbook photos, he showed 23 female and 25 male faces to two groups of subjects, each consisting of 19 women and 21 men. He asked one group to rate each face's attractiveness (1=low, 7=high) and the other group to rate each face's happiness (1=low, 7=high). When it was all over, Dennis had 80 response sheets (one from each subject) looking something like this:

attractiveness group

Check one: ___female _x_ male   14

Please indicate how attractive each face is, using a scale of 1 (very unattractive) to 7 (very attractive).

Face 1	3	Face 25	2
Face 2	5	Face 26	3
Face 3	2	Face 27	3
Face 4	2	Face 28	4
Face 5	1	Face 29	4
Face 6	6	Face 30	4
Face 7	7	Face 31	4
Face 8	6	Face 32	5
Face 9	4	Face 33	7
Face 10	4	Face 34	1
Face 11	3	Face 35	6
Face 12	4	Face 36	3
Face 13	3	Face 37	3
Face 14	4	Face 38	4
Face 15	5	Face 39	5
Face 16	2	Face 40	5
Face 17	1	Face 41	5
Face 18	1	Face 42	3
Face 19	4	Face 43	6
Face 20	4	Face 44	3
Face 21	5	Face 45	3
Face 22	7	Face 46	3
Face 23	5	Face 47	2
Face 24	4	Face 48	4

happiness group

Check one: _x_ female ___male   29

Please indicate how happy each face is, using a scale of 1 (very unhappy) to 7 (very happy).

Face 1	4	Face 25	4
Face 2	4	Face 26	3
Face 3	5	Face 27	3
Face 4	2	Face 28	6
Face 5	7	Face 29	4
Face 6	3	Face 30	1
Face 7	5	Face 31	4
Face 8	3	Face 32	7
Face 9	4	Face 33	6
Face 10	3	Face 34	5
Face 11	4	Face 35	7
Face 12	6	Face 36	4
Face 13	1	Face 37	6
Face 14	3	Face 38	4
Face 15	1	Face 39	1
Face 16	5	Face 40	4
Face 17	2	Face 41	2
Face 18	5	Face 42	4
Face 19	5	Face 43	2
Face 20	5	Face 44	3
Face 21	4	Face 45	5
Face 22	4	Face 46	3
Face 23	3	Face 47	3
Face 24	3	Face 48	2

(Notice that Dennis has numbered the response sheets in the upper right corner.) Let us put ourselves in Dennis's place and consider how to proceed. Eighty subjects times 48 faces gives us 3840 responses. Clearly we need to get these data into a computer in order to analyze them, but our first step requires thought rather than action. We need to figure out what's going into the computer and in what form.

First we'll list the variables and their values, and give each variable a name:

variable	values	variable name
subject number	1-40	subnum
subject sex	female, male	subsex
picture number	1-48	picnum
picture sex	female, male	picsex
group	happiness, attractiveness	group
rating	1-7	rating

Notice that we aren't treating happiness ratings and attractiveness ratings as two separate variables. Rather, we have only one rating variable, and a group variable to indicate what is being rated. (We'll discuss the pros and cons of doing things this way in Chapter 4.)

With 3840 responses, each consisting of six variables, we will need to enter 23040 values. To make matters worse, half of those values are strings. Fortunately, there are two things we can do to substantially reduce the typing burden. First, we can encode the string variables:

subsex	1=female, 2=male
picsex	1=female, 2=male
group	1=happiness, 2=attractiveness

Second, we can take advantage of the fact that there is a great deal of redundancy in the data. Every subject saw the same 48 pictures, so picnum and picsex will be the same for every subject. Similarly, a given subject's number, sex, and group are constant, so subnum, subsex, and group will be the same for all 48 of a subject's responses. With this in mind, we can set up the data set:

	subnum	subsex	group	picnum	picsex	rating
1						
2						
3						

Notice that the subject variables (subnum, subsex, group) are grouped together, as are the stimulus variables (picnum, picsex). This will speed things up, as you will see in a moment. Picking up the first response sheet, we see that it belongs to subject 1 in the attractiveness group, who is male. We enter these data this way:

	subnum	subsex	group	picnum	picsex	rating
1	1	2	2			
2						
3						

Because these values are constant for this subject, we can select the three cells we just filled in, copy them to the clipboard, and paste them into the next 47 rows.

	subnum	subsex	group	picnum	picsex	rating
1	1	2	2			
2	1	2	2			
3	1	2	2			
. . .						
48	1	2	2			

Now for the stimulus variables:

	subnum	subsex	group	picnum	picsex	rating
1	1	2	2	1	2	
2	1	2	2	2	2	
3	1	2	2	3	1	
. . .						
48	1	2	2	48	2	

Finally, the ratings:

	subnum	subsex	group	picnum	picsex	rating
1	1	2	2	1	2	4
2	1	2	2	2	2	1
3	1	2	2	3	1	3
. . .						
48	1	2	2	48	2	3

Now we put a checkmark on the response sheet we just entered and go on to the next: subject 2 in the attractiveness group, who is male. We enter the subject variables once and then paste them into the next 47 rows:

	subnum	subsex	group	picnum	picsex	rating
49	2	2	2			
50	2	2	2			
51	2	2	2			
. . .						
96	2	2	2			

Now we can fill in the stimulus variables by copying them from subject 1:

	subnum	subsex	group	picnum	picsex	rating
49	2	2	2	1	2	
50	2	2	2	2	2	
51	2	2	2	3	1	
. . .						
96	2	2	2	48	2	

Now the ratings:

	subnum	subsex	group	picnum	picsex	rating
49	2	2	2	1	2	4
50	2	2	2	2	2	2
51	2	2	2	3	1	6
. . .						
96	2	2	2	48	2	4

And so on, subject by subject. With a little planning, we were able to enter 23040 values with relatively little typing. The copy-and-paste approach not only speeds up data entry, but reduces our opportunities to make errors. Most data sets have some redundancy that can be exploited in this way.

The data from Dennis's study are in the computer, but we are not done with them. In Demonstration 2 we will check them for errors, and in Demonstration 8 we will do some analyses.

Data structures and operations

Chapter Outline

1. For some purposes we want each level of a categorical variable to correspond to a column in the data file: a *casewise* structure. For other purposes we want each level of a categorical variable to correspond to a row in the data file: a *scorewise* structure.

2. All computations can be understood in terms of *column operations*, *row operations*, and *by-operations*.

3. Statistical software will not perform certain operations, depending on the structure of the data. These limits reflect assumptions about data rather than computational impossibilities. The choice of data structure therefore depends on these limits and on what we want to do with the data.

4. Many data sets contain both casewise and scorewise elements.

5. We often need to change the structure of a data set. This can be done by hand or, sometimes, by computer.

6. Sometimes it is necessary to restrict an operation to a subset of the data. We can do this by specifying the cases or by using an *if* statement.

YOU HAVE SOME DATA. You know exactly what kinds of variables you have. You've determined exactly how each variable is to be encoded. Are you ready to enter your data? Not quite. There is usually one more important decision to make: how should the data be organized?

Suppose we have quarterly earnings for each of three companies. We could enter the data this way:

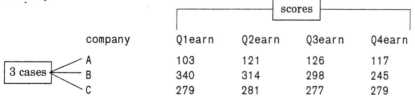

casewise structure

This illustrates what I will call *casewise structure*: each row of the data structure is a case (company A, B, or C), and all information about a given case is in one row.

Alternatively, we could enter the data this way:

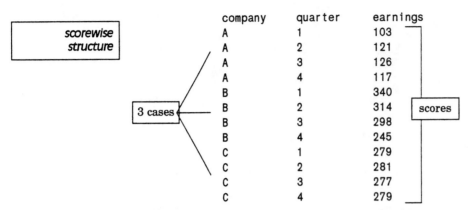

This is what I will call *scorewise structure*: each row of the data structure contains only one score, or value of a dependent variable. The information about a given case (company) is spread out over as many rows as there are scores; in this case four rows, because each case has a score (earnings) for each of four quarters.

Examine the above examples carefully and satisfy yourself that they contain the same data and differ only in *structure*, the way the data are arranged in rows and columns. If both structures provide exactly the same information, why does it matter which one we use? Because statistical software usually requires that the data be in a particular structure for a particular computation or operation. The structure we choose therefore depends on what we intend to do with the data.

4.1   Casewise and scorewise structures

Let's consider another example. Suppose we have a data set containing the sizes (in square kilometers) of black bears' territories measured in three different seasons (there are no winter measurements because black bears are inactive in the winter):

		------territory size-------		
bear id	sex	spring	summer	fall
1	1	50	70	30
2	2	67	85	41
3	2	74	93	38
4	1	46	72	34

(1=female,
2=male)

What are the variables in this data set? It depends on who you ask:

Computer's perspective		Our perspective	
bear id	(numeric)	bear id	(case identifier)
sex	(numeric)	sex	(independent)
spring territory size	(numeric)	season	(independent)
summer territory size	(numeric)	territory size	(dependent)
fall territory size	(numeric)		

The computer regards each column as a variable, and makes no distinctions among variables other than whether they are numbers or strings. We, on the other hand, make many distinctions among variables in terms of how they measure and their roles in our research. As bear researchers we want to know how the size of a bear's territory varies as a function of the season and the bear's sex.

The difference between these perspectives illustrates an important point: computers don't know anything about research design. The computer doesn't know that sex is an independent variable, or that territory size is a dependent variable, and – what's most important for our present purpose – it doesn't know that season is a variable at all, because it is confounded with the three columns of territory sizes rather than represented explicitly.

For each case we have a dependent measure (territory size) at each level of a categorical independent variable (season). When the data are in a casewise organization each level (spring, summer, fall) of the independent variable corresponds to a column in the data file. Measurements of the dependent variable (territory size) for each level of the independent variable go in a different column.

Here are the same data organized scorewise:

```
bear id        sex          season        territory size
1              1            1             50
1              1            2             70
1              1            3             30
2              2            1             67
2              2            2             85
2              2            3             41
3              2            1             74
3              2            2             93
3              2            3             38
4              1            1             46
4              1            2             72
4              1            3             34
                            (1=spring,
                            2=summer,
                            3=fall)
```

Now the computer sees the data more or less as we do:

Computer's perspective		Our perspective	
bear id	(numeric)	bear id	(case identifier)
sex	(numeric)	sex	(independent)
season	(numeric)	season	(independent)
territory size	(numeric)	territory size	(dependent)

The data are the same in both structures. For each case we have a dependent measure (territory size) at each level of a categorical independent variable (season). The difference is that when the data are organized scorewise each level of the categorical variable corresponds to a row in the data file. Bear id is a variable to the computer and a case identifier to us; we need it to show that, for example, the first three lines in the data set constitute a single case, i.e. bear no. 1.

As this example illustrates, the choice between casewise and scorewise structure boils down to whether we want a categorical independent variable to be represented implicitly, embedded in two or more columns of dependent measures (casewise) or explicitly, with each level of the independent variable for each case constituting a separate observation (scorewise). This will help us to develop some guidelines for making this choice.

4.2   Using casewise and scorewise data

Suppose we have the casewise bear data and want to compute the mean territory size for each bear. We can create a new variable, meansize, by adding the three size values in each row and dividing the sum by three:

bear id	sex	------------ territory size ------------			
		spring	summer	fall	meansize
1	1	50	70	30	50.0
2	2	67	85	41	64.3
3	2	74	93	38	68.3
4	1	46	72	34	50.7
	(1=female, 2=male)				

row operations

For bear 1 we compute (50+70+30)/3=50, and so on for the other bears. This computation is a *row operation*: all the values needed for the computation are found in a single row, and the result is put in the same row.

column operations

If we want to know the mean spring territory size for the bears in our sample, we compute (50+67+74+46)/4=59.25. This computation is a *column operation*: all the values needed for the computation are found in a single column. (Note, however, that the result does not become part of the data set for the simple reason that there is no appropriate place for it. If we put the mean in the spring column (from which it was computed) then that column would contain four territory sizes and one mean territory size. Furthermore, the mean would occupy a fifth row in the data set. The first four rows correspond to bears; what would the fifth row correspond to?)

If we want to know the overall mean territory size for all bears in our sample, we can compute the mean territory size for each bear (a row operation) and then compute the mean of the row means (a column operation): (50.0+64.3+68.3+50.7)/4=58.3. Equivalently, we can compute the mean territory size in each season (a column operation) and then compute the mean of the column means (a row operation): (59.25+80.00+35.75)/3=58.3.

Now try doing the same things with the data in the scorewise organization. All the territory sizes are in a single column, so you can find the overall mean territory size with a single column operation, but that's it. Does this mean that the scorewise structure is less useful?

To answer this, consider some other things we'd like to get from the data, such as the mean spring territory size for females. First we have to identify the appropriate data:

bear id	sex	spring	summer	fall
1	1	50 ⇦	70	30
2	2	67	85	41
3	2	74	93	38
4	1	46 ⇦	72	34

The mean spring territory size for females is (50+46)/2=48. Similarly, to find the mean summer territory size for males, the data we need are:

bear id	sex	spring	summer	fall
1	1	50	70	30
2	2	67	85 ⇦	41
3	2	74	93 ⇦	38
4	1	46	72	34

The mean summer territory size for males is (85+93)/2=89. And so on. We cannot compute these means with a simple row or column operation. Could we do it with the scorewise data? Let's try it. To find the mean spring territory size for females we have to identify the appropriate data:

bear id	sex	season	territory size
1	1	1	50 ⇦
1	1	2	70
1	1	3	30
2	2	1	67
2	2	2	85
2	2	3	41
3	2	1	74
3	2	2	93
3	2	3	38
4	1	1	46 ⇦
4	1	2	72
4	1	3	34

(1=spring,
2=summer,
3=fall)

This is no better: the data we need are not by themselves in a row or column. Perhaps if we sorted the data differently?

bear id	sex	season	territory size
1	1	1	50 ⇦
4	1	1	46 ⇦
1	1	2	70
4	1	2	72
1	1	3	30
4	1	3	34
2	2	1	67
3	2	1	74
2	2	2	85
3	2	2	93
2	2	3	41
3	2	3	38

(1=spring,
2=summer,
3=fall)

The data we need are now next to one another, but we still cannot find their mean with a simple row or column operation, and this will be true now matter how we sort the data.

> **by operations**

This example demonstrates the need for a third kind of operation on a data set, which we will call a *by operation*. The operations we performed to find the mean female spring territory size were neither row nor column operations; rather, we computed mean territory size *by sex and season*. "By sex" means "once for each unique value of the variable sex." Thus "by sex and season" means "once for each unique combination of the variables sex and season," so we computed the mean of all values of *size* with the same combination of *sex* and *season*. There are six such combinations, corresponding to the six cells of the summary table below:

mean territory size	spring	summer	fall	overall
females	48.0	71.0	32.0	50.33
males	70.5	89.0	39.5	66.33
overall	59.25	80.00	35.75	58.33

We can summarize the three kinds of operations on a data set as follows:

Column operation: An operation performed on all the values in a column, such as finding the sum, mean, standard deviation, etc.

Row operation: An operation performed within each row on the values of some or all variables, such as finding the sum, difference, mean, etc.

By operation: An operation performed separately for each value of the *by-variable* or for each combination of by-variables.

4.3   Software limitations

Why all this fuss about structures and operations? After all, we can get whatever we need from any kind of data set. We can, but our software usually cannot. It is much less flexible than we are, and to use it we must work within its limitations. In a nutshell those limitations are as follows: Different statistics packages are willing to do different row, column, and by-operations with different structures.

Consider the bear data once more. We were able to compute the mean territory sizes by sex and season from the casewise data, but most software cannot, because season is not a variable in the casewise structure:

```
> compute mean of size, by sex season
***unknown variable "season"***
```

This is frustrating, because, as we saw earlier, we understand that what the computer thinks of as the variables spring, summer, and fall are in fact the levels, or values, of the variable season. For some purposes, some software will allow us to communicate this understanding by defining a variable in terms of two or more columns, e.g.:

```
> define variable season, levels 1=spring 2=summer 3=fall
```

In other cases we can simply name the columns and the software will treat them as the levels of a single variable, e.g.:

```
> anova oneway spring summer fall
```

If our software won't do this, we must enter the data scorewise. Now both sex and season are explicit variables, and the software can compute the means using a by-operation:

```
> compute mean of size, by sex season
```

Many people first encounter these structure/operation limitations when trying to do a t-test. Every program seems to have a different perspective on t-tests, and it can get confusing. Suppose we have data from a simple memory experiment in which all subjects read the same list of ten words, and the next day are asked to recall the words. A week later, the same subjects are again asked to recall the words. We want to know whether the independent variable (length of retention interval – one day / one week) has an effect on the dependent variable (number of words recalled). Retention interval varies within subjects, so this calls for a t-test for related samples:[1] does the mean number of words recalled after one day differ significantly from the mean number of words recalled after one week? To answer this we could enter the data casewise:

```
sub_id    1day     1week
1         7        3
2         9        5
3         6        3
4         6        2
```

Now we can ask for a t-test:

```
> compute t (paired) 1day = 1week

Paired t test
number of cases:    4
degrees of freedom: 3

variable    mean      s.e.        t       p
1day        7.00      .71
1week       3.25      .63
diff.       3.75      .25         15      0.0006
```

Notice that we got a related-samples t-test even though we didn't explicitly ask for it. Most software assumes that in casewise data the variables all contain measurements of the same cases. Could we arrange these data scorewise? Sure:

```
sub_id    recall     interval
1         7          1
2         9          1
3         6          1
4         6          1
1         3          2
2         5          2
3         3          2
4         2          2
```

To do a related-samples test with the data arranged this way requires a by-operation. This could easily be done, but most software won't do it, reflecting the strength of the assumption just mentioned.

Now imagine a slightly different experiment. One group of subjects reads a list of 10 words and another group hears the same list of words read to them. The next day all subjects are asked to recall the words. We want to know whether the independent variable (type of presentation – visual or auditory) has an effect on the dependent variable (number of words recalled). Type of presentation varies between the two groups of subjects, so this calls for a t-test for two independent samples: does the mean number of words recalled by the visual group differ significantly from the mean number of words recalled by the auditory group? To answer this we could enter the data casewise:

---

[1] Also known as the t-test for correlated or paired samples.

```
visual      auditory
7           6
5           7
8           3
```

Now we can ask for a t-test:

```
> compute t (unpaired) visual = auditory
Two-sample t test
equal variances assumed
number of cases / visual:  3
number of cases / auditory:      3
degrees of freedom: 4
```

variable	mean	s.e.	t	p
visual	6.67	0.882		
auditory	5.33	1.202		
diff.	1.33	1.491	0.894	0.4216

Notice that we had explicitly to tell the software that the two columns mentioned represent independent samples. Had we not done so, the software would have assumed they were related samples. This is fine, but for an independent t-test some software will insist that the data be scorewise:

```
subject       presentation      recall
1             1                 7
2             1                 5
3             1                 8
4             2                 6
5             2                 7
6             2                 3
              (1=visual,
               2=auditory)
```

With scorewise data we frame our request differently:

```
> compute t (unpaired) recall, groups are presentation=1,2
```

The output will be exactly what we got in the last example.

Doing this test with casewise data required three column operations: finding n, the mean, and sum of squares for each of two variables. Doing exactly the same test with scorewise data required a by-operation. Some software will do this test either way and some only the second way.

These examples will suffice to illustrate a general rule of thumb about statistical software. For most purposes, repeated measures of the same cases are expected to be in separate columns (casewise structure), and measures of different cases are expected to be in different rows (scorewise structure).

4.4   Mixed structures

So far we have been treating the casewise/scorewise distinction as an either/or proposition, but in reality a data set will often contain elements of both structures. We can get a simple example by combining the designs of the two memory experiments. One group reads the list of words and the other hears it read aloud. Both groups are tested for recall the next day and again a week later. We want to know three things: (1) Does the type of exposure (visual/auditory) to the words have an effect on number of words recalled? (2) Does the length of the retention interval (1 day/1 week) have an effect on number of words recalled? (3) If either of the independent variables has a significant effect, does it interact with the other independent variable? Retention is a within-subjects variable and presentation is a between-groups variable, so we will do a two-way analysis of variance for a mixed design. How should we arrange the data? If we follow our rule of thumb they will look like this:

sub_id	exposure	recall1	recall2
1	1	7	4
2	1	5	3
3	1	8	4
4	2	6	2
5	2	7	3
6	2	3	1

The between-groups variable (exposure) is scorewise, while the within-subjects variable (retention interval) is casewise.

4.5   Changing structure

What happens if we choose the wrong structure for our data? What should we do if we need the data organized one way for some purposes and the other way for other purposes? The news is reasonably good: you do not have to enter the data twice. There are two ways to change the structure of your data. One involves a good deal of cutting and pasting, which is tedious and error prone but usually beats data entry. The other way is to let the software do it, but not all software has this capability.

The cut-and-paste method. Suppose we have data like the following:

state	pop_1970	pop_1980	pop_1990	(in 1000s)
Alabama	3,444	3,894	4,048	
Alaska	303	402	553	
Arizona	1,775	2,718	3,679	
Arkansas	1,923	2,286	2,354	
etc.				

If we need to change the data set from this casewise organization to a scorewise one, the first step is to identify the variables. From our perspective – not the computer's – they are:

state	[case identifier]
year	[independent variable]
population	[dependent variable]

These variables will define the columns in the scorewise structure. Now we will move the data around. To make it easier to see where the value in a given cell goes, we'll replace the population numbers with codes that designate the cells of the data set:

state	pop_1970	pop_1980	pop_1990
Alabama	1.70	1.80	1.90
Alaska	2.70	2.80	2.90
Arizona	3.70	3.80	3.90
Arkansas	4.70	4.80	4.90
etc.			

The code 1.70 indicates the first case (Alabama) and the year 1970; 3.90 indicates the third case (Arizona) and the year 1990. (Note that this is for illustration only, and is not part of the process of restructuring the data set.) Because the independent variable (year) is not represented explicitly in the casewise data, the first step is to make a year variable:

	state	pop_1970	pop_1980	pop_1990	year
1	Alabama	1.70	1.80	1.90	
2	Alaska	2.70	2.80	2.90	
3	Arizona	3.70	3.80	3.90	
4	Arkansas	4.70	4.80	4.90	

The next question is: how many columns (i.e. levels of the independent variable) are going to be rearranged into one column? In this case there are three, so we need each case identifier (state) to appear three times:

	state	pop_1970	pop_1980	pop_1990	year
1	Alabama	1.70	1.80	1.90	
2	Alaska	2.70	2.80	2.90	
3	Arizona	3.70	3.80	3.90	
4	Arkansas	4.70	4.80	4.90	
5	Alabama				
6	Alaska				
7	Arizona				
8	Arkansas				
9	Alabama				
10	Alaska				
11	Arizona				
12	Arkansas				

Now we can fill in the year variable:

	state	pop_1970	pop_1980	pop_1990	year
1	Alabama	1.70	1.80	1.90	1970
2	Alaska	2.70	2.80	2.90	1970
3	Arizona	3.70	3.80	3.90	1970
4	Arkansas	4.70	4.80	4.90	1970
5	Alabama				1980
6	Alaska				1980
7	Arizona				1980
8	Arkansas				1980
9	Alabama				1990
10	Alaska				1990
11	Arizona				1990
12	Arkansas				1990

Now we can collapse the three columns containing the dependent variable (population) into one. The population values in 1970_pop are where they belong (according to the year column), so we will leave them there, rename that column, and move the other columns of population values into it:

	state	pop_1970	pop_1980	pop_1990	year
1	Alabama	1.70	1.80	1.90	1970
2	Alaska	2.70	2.80	2.90	1970
3	Arizona	3.70	3.80	3.90	1970
4	Arkansas	4.70	4.80	4.90	1970
5	Alabama	1.80	←		1980
6	Alaska	2.80			1980
7	Arizona	3.80			1980
8	Arkansas	4.80			1980
9	Alabama				1990
10	Alaska				1990
11	Arizona				1990
12	Arkansas				1990

The 1980 populations are moved (or copied) as a block to the appropriate place in the new population column, and likewise the 1990 populations:

	state	pop_1970	pop_1980	pop_1990	year
1	Alabama	1.70	1.80	1.90	1970
2	Alaska	2.70	2.80	2.90	1970
3	Arizona	3.70	3.80	3.90	1970
4	Arkansas	4.70	4.80	4.90	1970
5	Alabama	1.80			1980
6	Alaska	2.80			1980
7	Arizona	3.80			1980
8	Arkansas	4.80			1980
9	Alabama	1.90	←		1990
10	Alaska	2.90			1990
11	Arizona	3.90			1990
12	Arkansas	4.90			1990

Finally, we can delete the columns that are no longer needed:

	state	population	year
1	Alabama	1.70	1970
2	Alaska	2.70	1970
3	Arizona	3.70	1970
4	Arkansas	4.70	1970
5	Alabama	1.80	1980
6	Alaska	2.80	1980
7	Arizona	3.80	1980
8	Arkansas	4.80	1980
9	Alabama	1.90	1990
10	Alaska	2.90	1990
11	Arizona	3.90	1990
12	Arkansas	4.90	1990

What if we need to go the other way (i.e. scorewise to casewise)? No problem. Here are some scorewise sales data for Pretty Good Gravel Company's three grades of gravel:

```
grade           region          tons
fine            east            1024
fine            central         3097
fine            west            2356
medium          east            4088
medium          central         4993
medium          west            4721
coarse          east            3319
coarse          central         3681
coarse          west            3645
```

As before, we begin by identifying the variables:

```
grade           [case identifier]
region          [independent variable]
tons            [dependent variable]
```

In the previous example we had to break apart the independent and dependent variables; this time we have to put them together. For each region we want a column containing the number of tons sold. This means we need to sort the data so that the tons values for each region will be together (again we will replace the dependent measures with cell designators):

```
> sort on region grade, ascending
grade           region          tons
fine            east            1.e
medium          east            2.e
coarse          east            3.e
fine            central         1.c
medium          central         2.c
coarse          central         3.c
fine            west            1.w
medium          west            2.w
coarse          west            3.w
```

The first step is to make the new columns we will need:

	grade	region	tons/ east	tons/ central	tons/ west
1	fine	east	1.e		
2	medium	east	2.e		
3	coarse	east	3.e		
4	fine	central	1.c		
5	medium	central	2.c		
6	coarse	central	3.c		
7	fine	west	1.w		
8	medium	west	2.w		
9	coarse	west	3.w		

Notice that we've renamed the tons column to tons/east. Now we can start moving data:

	grade	region	tons/east	tons/central	tons/west
1	fine	east	1.e	1.c	
2	medium	east	2.e	2.c	
3	coarse	east	3.e	3.c	
4	fine	central	1.c		
5	medium	central	2.c		
6	coarse	central	3.c		
7	fine	west	1.w		
8	medium	west	2.w		
9	coarse	west	3.w		

	grade	region	tons/east	tons/central	tons/west
1	fine	east	1.e	1.c	1.w
2	medium	east	2.e	2.c	2.w
3	coarse	east	3.e	3.c	3.w
4	fine	central	1.c		
5	medium	central	2.c		
6	coarse	central	3.c		
7	fine	west	1.w		
8	medium	west	2.w		
9	coarse	west	3.w		

Again notice that the data are moved in blocks. Now we can get rid of the region variable and the extra rows:

	grade	tons/east	tons/central	tons/west	
1	fine	1.e	1.c	1.w	
2	medium	2.e	2.c	2.w	
3	coarse	3.e	3.c	3.w	

Done. If you want to convince yourself that no data are lost in the transformation from one structure to the other, turn this back into a scorewise data set.

The software method. Some software will take care of the cutting and pasting for you. However, it's not quite as simple as telling the computer to change the structure of the data. You have to tell it what to do with each of the existing variables and what new variables to make. If you can use the cut-and-paste method, it shouldn't be hard to instruct the software. To illustrate, we'll repeat the examples we just did.

In the state populations example, we begin with a casewise-oriented data set containing

state	[case identifier]
pop_1970	[dep. var. (pop) for 1st level of ind. var. (year)]
pop_1980	[dep. var. (pop) for 2nd level of ind. var. (year)]
pop_1990	[dep. var. (pop) for 3rd level of ind. var. (year)]

and we want to wind up with

state	[case identifier]
year	[independent variable]
population	[dependent variable]

Here's what we tell the computer:

```
> restructure scorewise / id=state
 / grouping var=year, values=1970, 1980, 1990
 / dep var=population, prefix=pop_
```

Such a command tells the computer how to break apart the independent and dependent variable: The dependent values are in the pop_ columns, and in the new scorewise data set these values should be in cases whose year values are the same as the suffixes of the pop_ column names. We also tell it that state is a case identifier.

In the gravel sales example, we begin with a scorewise data set containing

grade	[case identifier]
region	[independent variable]
tons	[dependent variable]

and we want to wind up with

grade	[case identifier]
tons_east	[dep. measure (tons) for 1st level of ind. var. (region)]
tons_central	[dep. measure (tons) for 2nd level of ind. var. (region)]
tons_west	[dep. measure (tons) for 3rd level of ind. var. (region)]

Here's what we tell the computer:

```
> restructure casewise / id=grade
 / grouping var=region, values=east, central, west
 / dep var=tons, prefix=tons_
```

This tells the computer how to combine the independent and dependent variables: The dependent values are in the tons column, and in the new structure these values should be in separate columns for each level of the independent variable. The values of the independent variable are in the region column, and in the new structure these values should be represented in the names of the columns containing the dependent measures.

Reorganizing a data set can be confusing, regardless of the method you use. Don't try to do it in your head. List the variables you have, identify them as we have done in the examples, list and identify the variables you want, and figure out what will become what. Whatever you do, SAVE YOUR DATA before moving data around. It is true that restructuring is a reversible process, but only if it's done right. If you make a mistake you will have a data set that isn't what you want and can't be restored to its original state, and you will be glad that you saved the original data set.

4.6   Being selective

Sometimes we don't want to use the whole data set in a particular operation. Imagine that we have just entered the data from an experiment when we discover that on the last day the experimental apparatus was malfunctioning. The data collected on that day are probably no good. We can solve this problem in two ways.

Specific range. If the malfunction affected every variable we would probably get rid of the data in question. We look in the experiment log and find that subjects 73 through 88 participated in the experiment on the last day. Then, if there is one row per subject, we can

```
> sort on subject_id, ascending
> delete rows 73-88
```

If, on the other hand, the malfunction affected only some of the variables – say, X but not Y – we might decide to keep the data (perhaps we have hopes of being able to correct the affected data) but exclude those cases from certain operations.

```
> sort on subject_id, ascending
> compute mean of Y
> compute mean of X, rows 1-72
```

By specifying a range of rows, we tell the software where to find the data we want it to use. There are times when this method of restriction is just the ticket. The drawback, of course, is that we must know the row numbers of the cases we want to include or exclude, and those cases must all be in a continuous range of rows. Sometimes there is a more powerful approach.

Conditional inclusion. IF is a very big word. We can use it to delete data we don't want:

```
> delete all vars if subject_id > 72
```

Likewise, we can specify which cases to include in a computation:

```
> compute mean of Y
> compute mean of X if subject_id < 73
```

The advantage of *if* is that when there is something in the data set that we can use as the basis for including only certain cases, we don't need to bother with row numbers, and we don't need to sort the data in any particular way. By using *if* we tell the software "Perform this operation, but include a case in that operation only if it meets a certain condition."

For example, we might have some data on skin cancer patients:

name	date of birth	date diagnosed	current status	method of treatment
Felix Gonzalez	07-12-23	10-17-94	1	1
Harold Brown	01-03-36	04-21-89	1	2
Alice Murphy	12-18-34	07-03-92	2	2
Jane Hanson	09-14-41	05-20-96	3	2
Arthur Needleman	02-28-31	11-30-88	1	1
Martha Pratt	09-09-49	08-19-95	2	1
Ellen Davis	08-16-42	12-21-97	1	2
Glenn Horowitz	03-14-51	02-11-96	2	2

(1=remission;
2=limited metastasis;
3=extensive metastasis)

Suppose we are setting up a clinical trial of a new treatment, and we need to recruit patients who currently have limited metastasis. Using *if*, we can generate a list of all (and only) those patients who fit the bill:

```
> list name if current_status = 2
Alice Murphy
Martha Pratt
Glenn Horowitz
```

The real beauty of conditional inclusion is that we can make the condition (the part after *if*) very specific or detailed. Suppose the eligibility criteria for the clinical trial are a bit more specific: we need patients who underwent treatment 2 and currently have moderate metastasis.

```
> list name if current_status = 2 & treatment = 2
Alice Murphy
Glenn Horowitz
```

Suppose instead that we need patients who were diagnosed more than ten years ago or who are over 65 years old:

```
> list name if dx_date < 06-30-89 OR d_o_b < 06-30-34
Felix Gonzalez
Harold Brown
Arthur Needleman
```

Gonzalez meets the birth date criterion, Brown meets the diagnosis date criterion, and Needleman meets both criteria. Finally, suppose our criteria combine *and* and *or*:

```
> list name if treatment=1 OR (treatment=2 & d_o_b>06-30-49)
Felix Gonzalez
Arthur Needleman
Martha Pratt
Glenn Horowitz
```

Notice that parentheses are used to prevent ambiguity. If

A stands for "treatment = 1"
B stands for "treatment = 2"
C stands for "d_o_b > 06-30-49"

then the condition we specified in the above command is

A or (B and C)

You should convince yourself that this is not the same as

(A or B) and C

and that therefore

A or B and C

is ambiguous.

Selectivity is an important and powerful tool of data analysis, but bear in mind that it does not apply to everything. You can't sort only some of the cases; you have to sort the whole data set. The same goes for reorienting data, and for any other procedure that changes or rearranges data, such as merging (see ch. 7) and collapsing (see ch. 8).

4.7   Exercises

1. Here is the total monthly rainfall (in inches) for three cities:

month	New York	Chicago	Los Angeles
Jan	3.3	1.9	2.8
Feb	3.1	1.6	2.4
Mar	3.9	2.8	2.0
Apr	3.7	3.8	0.8
May	4.2	3.2	0.1
Jun	3.3	4.1	0.0
Jul	4.1	4.0	0.0
Aug	4.1	3.5	0.1
Sep	3.6	3.1	0.2
Oct	3.3	2.7	0.3
Nov	4.2	2.9	1.5
Dec	3.6	2.6	1.7

a. What form (casewise or scorewise) are these data in?
b. What is the total annual rainfall in New York? What kind of operation (row or column or by) did you use to compute this number?
c. What is the mean monthly rainfall in Los Angeles? What kind of operation did you use to compute this?
d. What is the mean rainfall, in these three cities, in February? What kind of operation did you use to compute this?

2. Put the rainfall data into the other form.

a. What is the total annual rainfall in Chicago? What kind of operation did you use to compute this?

b. What is the mean rainfall, in these three cities, in November? What kind of operation did you use to compute this?

3. Here is the record of the number of points scored by each member of a basketball team in each game:

name	game	points
Belinda	1	7
Melinda	1	12
Melissa	1	4
Clarissa	1	9
Ruth	1	10
Belinda	2	8
Melinda	2	14
Melissa	2	8
Clarissa	2	7
Ruth	2	12
Belinda	3	10
Melinda	3	14
Melissa	3	9
Clarissa	3	9
Ruth	3	11

a. What form are these data in?

b. What is the mean number of points per player per game for the season? What kind of operation did you use to compute this?

c. What is Melissa's mean number of points per game? What kind of operation did you use to compute this?

4. Put the basketball data into the other form.

a. How many points did the team score in game 2? What kind of operation did you use to compute this?

b. What is Melinda's mean number of points per game? What kind of operation did you use to compute this?

5. The Amalgamated Shoehorn Co. makes three models of shoehorn: the #7 Steel Standard, the #12b Steel Narrow, and the #66 Long-handled Standard. Make up a year's worth of monthly sales figures (i.e. a number ($) for each model for each month), arranging the data in the appropriate forms to do each of the following:

a. Find the total sales for each month using only column operations.

b. Find the total annual sales of each model using only column operations.

c. Find Amalgamated's mean monthly sales using only by-operations.

d. Find the total sales for each month using only row operations.

e. Find the total annual sales of each model using only row operations.

f. Find Amalgamated's total annual sales (i.e. of all models) using only row and column operations.

g. Find Amalgamated's total annual sales using only column operations.

6. Repeat exercises 1-5 using a computer. Depending on the software you are using, you probably will not be able to do all of the things you did by hand. However, you will be able to compute all the sums and means the exercises ask for. The point of this exercise is not so much to answer the questions as to discover what your software will and will not do and how to arrange your data to be able to compute what you need within the software's limitations.

Checking Data

Chapter Outline

There is no way to be certain that all our data are correct, but there are some useful things we can do to minimize errors.

1. Brute force methods:
    - proofreading
    - double data entry
2. Intelligent methods:
    - detecting improbable values
    - detecting impossible values
    - detecting inconsistent values

LOOKING FOR TYPOGRAPHICAL ERRORS in text is not quite as much fun as cleaning the toilet, but at least it's not hard; even a computer can spot the errors in

```
It is a pleasure to rexommend Herman Sherman gor your
graduate [program in Frozen Foods Management.
```

But who can spot the errors in data?

```
7      13     0.41    128
6      61     0.39    147
8      12     0.46   -139
7      15     43      162
```

Because not all sequences of letters are words, word processors can have spelling checkers. But because any sequence of digits is a number, statistical software can't have data checkers. Since the software can't do it, we must.

5.1   Brute force methods

Nothing is guaranteed to catch any and all errors in our data, but there are times when we need to be certain – or however close to certain we can come – that we've got them all and that our data are clean. At such times, we have two options. One is to proofread the data, by checking every value in the data file against the data sheet it came from. This goes much faster, and is more accurate, if two people work together, one reading aloud from the data file and the other following silently in the data sheet, or vice versa.

The other option is for two people to enter the data separately, or for one person to enter the data twice. The likelihood of a given error occurring both times is very small, so if the two files are identical they are very likely error free; if they are not identical , one has an error. Of course, we don't know which.

Double data entry is a lot of work, but file comparison is not. We don't need anything fancier than DOS's FC (File Compare) utility. Suppose we have entered the same data twice (it is best to make text files):

comparing data files

data 1				data 2		
24	35	9.3		24	35	9.3
2	8	8.9		2	9	8.9
25	54	7.8		25	54	7.8
74	6	9.1		74	6	9.1
53	23	8.2		53	23	8.3
87	60	8.7		87	60	8.7

At the DOS prompt (C:\>) we ask FC to compare these two files:

```
C:\>fc\n data1.txt data2.txt

Comparing files data1.txt and data2.txt

****** data1.txt
      1:    24    35    9.3
      2:     2     8    8.9
      3:    25    54    7.8
****** data2.txt
      1:    24    35    9.3
      2:     2     9    8.9
      3:    25    54    7.8
******

****** data1.txt
      4:    74     6    9.1
      5:    53    23    8.2
      6:    87    60    8.7
****** data2.txt
      4:    74     6    9.1
      5:    53    23    8.3
      6:    87    60  · 8.7
******
```

Wherever FC finds a discrepancy between the two files, it shows us that line, from each file, plus the lines above and below. In the output above, FC has found a discrepancy in the second variable in line 2 and another in the third variable in line 5. It is now a simple matter to check our original data sheets to find and fix the error.

5.2   Intelligent methods

If the brute force methods weren't so tedious, there would be no need to go any farther. But tedious they are, and when a data set is big and/or time and labor are limited, we may need to forget about near-certainty and settle for finding most of the biggest errors.

Improbable values. Consider again the two examples at the beginning of this chapter from another perspective. There's nothing wrong with x, g, or [in and of themselves. Rather, the contexts in which they occur make them errors. We can say that x doesn't belong in a word that is obviously meant to be *recommend*; can we say that the 61 in the second column is an error because 6 doesn't belong in a number that is obviously meant to be... who knows? There's no way to know what a number is supposed to be, and therefore no way to spot a digit that doesn't belong.

Still, it may strike us that 61 is unlike the other values of the second variable; likewise that 43 is unlike other values of the third variable, and so on. Now we are asking if we can spot an error by looking at a number in the context of other values of the same variable. The answer is yes – sometimes. If the 61 looks fishy we might go back to our data sheets and find that it should be 16; a simple and common reversal error. Likewise we might find we had left off a decimal point in front of 43.

To put it a little more formally, we are looking for, and checking, numbers that seem improbable in the context of a particular variable. There's nothing improbable about 43, but it seems improbable in the context of a variable whose other values are between 0 and 1.

There are systematic ways of looking for improbable values. Suppose we want to check the values of variable Q.

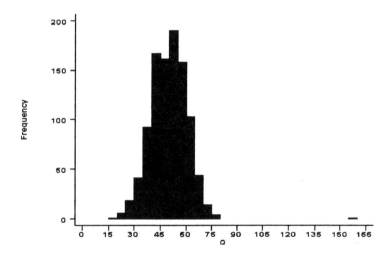

Graphs can be useful for detecting improbable values.

This histogram shows the distribution of Q. The values are all between roughly 15 and 80 except for that tiny bar way off to the right, which shows that there's at least one value somewhere between 150 and 165. Another way to see this is with a box plot.

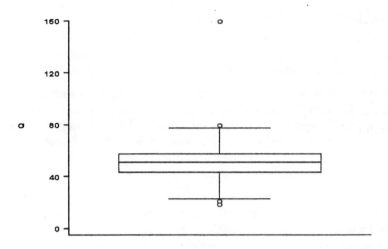

The box plot shows that the far-out bar in the histogram probably contains only one case (unless there are two or more cases with exactly the same extreme value, which seems unlikely). Why is this case's value improbable? Again, it is not the value itself, but the context as well, that makes us suspicious. Specifically, as both graphs show, Q is approximately normally distributed. The suspect value is many standard deviations from the center of the distribution, which makes it extremely unlikely from a purely probabilistic point of view. Does this mean it's an error? Not necessarily, but it would be wise to check. How?

We first need to know which case this improbable value belongs to. An easy way to do this is to sort and list the data; the extreme value will be at one end of the list.

> sort on Q, descending

> list case_id, Q

	case_id	Q
1.	451	159.0395
2.	720	78.8682
3.	934	77.2960
4.	931	76.5032
5.	842	75.6736
6.	273	74.6622
7.	380	74.4561
8.	527	74.4054
9.	539	74.1340
10.	435	74.0522

etc.

> There are several ways to find which case an improbable value is in.

There it is: case number 451. Since we were smart and gave every case an id number, all we have to do is find data sheet (or questionnaire, etc.) 451. If for some reason we neglected this important step, we would have to

> list case 1   [note that case 1 means the first case; because the cases are sorted in descending order of Q, the first case will be the one we're after]

Q	X	Y	Z
159.0395	407.15	89.9	201.08

and look through the sheets for one matching these values of X, Y, and Z. We don't look for a matching value of Q because we suspect it might not be there.

Once we have found the relevant data sheet, we check the value of variable Q. If it is different from the value in the data file, we correct the error and move on. What if it's not an error? In that case we have what's called an *outlier*, a value that lies outside of the range of most or all of the other values.

Outliers are often legitimate measurements. Someone who lives to the age of 110 is an outlier; the wealthiest person in the world is an outlier; Joe DiMaggio's 56-game hitting streak was an outlier. Outliers can also be questionable measurements. Suppose 10 children are given a puzzle to put together. Nine of them take between five and six minutes and one takes an hour. This measurement is accurate – there's nothing wrong with the clock – but it's questionable whether it measures the same thing in the case of the tenth child as it measures in the other nine. This child may have a visual defect, or may have fallen asleep, or may not have understood the instructions to solve the puzzle as quickly as possible.

outliers

Impossible values. You may have noticed that our definition of improbable was based entirely on the distribution of values and made no reference to what was being measured. 159.0395 seemed an unlikely value of Q because it was so far beyond the other values, despite the fact that I never said what Q was. Suppose I tell you that Q is in fact the ages of 1000 adult humans. Knowing what Q measures provides another important context, and now we have another reason for suspecting that 159.0395 is an error: humans just don't live that long.

Both categorical and quantitative variables can only have certain values; anything else is an error.

Knowing what a variable measures usually gives us a way of spotting improbable or implausible values, and often allows us to identify impossible values. There are three kinds of impossible value.

Out-of-range value. An age of 159 is very improbable, but an age of -7 is logically impossible. When the range of a variable is finite, some values are impossible, and if we find such a value in our data we have found an error. Many variables, such as age, weight, and elapsed time, are restricted to positive numbers. Other variables, such as velocity, probability, and bowling scores, are limited at both ends. The easiest way to look for range violations is to ask for the minimum and maximum values of a variable:

```
> compute min max of golfscor

minimum = 15
maximum = 95
```

A golfer's score is the number of strokes s/he takes to complete the course, and the player with the lowest score wins. Given 18 holes, a perfect score would be 18, so 15 is impossible. To correct the error we would use the same procedure we followed earlier: find the case id number by sorting and listing, check the data sheet, and correct the data file.

Range violations can also occur in categorical variables. Perhaps you've asked 200 people whether they plan to vote in the upcoming election, and you encode their answers as

vote	label
0	no
1	yes
2	undecided
9	no response

To see if you made any data entry errors, tabulate the variable:

```
> tabulate row=vote
```

```
vote         freq.    %
no           50       25
yes          120      60
undecided    20       10
3            1        .5
no response  9        4.5
```

The 3 appears without a label because there is no label for it; it can only be an error.

Wrong value type. We can use golf again to illustrate the second kind of impossible value. A golf score must be at least 18, and given what it measures it also had better be an integer: you can take 73 strokes or 74 strokes, but not 73.4 strokes. Any counting variable will have this restriction. One way to find violations is to get the sum of the values. If it's not an integer then at least one case has a non-integral value. If it is an integer, there could be two or more non-integers that add up to an integer (e.g. 73.4, 73.6).

Another method is a bit like using a mirror to find a vampire (they have no reflection). Suppose we define the function round(x) to equal x rounded to the nearest integer, so round(5.3)=5, round(5.7)=6, and so on. This function (and others like it) has a useful property. When x is a non-integer, round(x)≠ x, whereas when x is an integer, round(x)=x. From this it follows that for non-integers

$$x - \text{round}(x) \neq 0$$

while for integers

$$x - \text{round}(x) = 0$$

If we have a variable whose values should all be integers, we can test them as follows:

    a) round each value
    b) subtract each rounded value from the corresponding original value
    c) compute the mean difference; it should be zero.

We have a data set containing golf scores:

	case_id	score		
1	1	78		
2	2	91		
3	3	77.8		
4	4	84		
5	5	82.3		

To test for non-integer scores we round each score:

```
> create rscore, values = round(score)
```

Now we have:

	case_id	score	rscore	
1	1	78	78	
2	2	91	91	
3	3	77.8	78	
4	4	84	84	
5	5	82.3	82	

Then we take the difference:

```
> create diff, values = score - rscore
```

This gives us:

	case_id	score	rscore	diff
1	1	78	78	0
2	2	91	91	0
3	3	77.8	78	-0.2
4	4	84	84	0
5	5	82.3	82	0.3

Finally,

```
> compute mean of diff
var diff      n              mean
              1000           0.02
```

the fact that the mean difference is not zero tells us there's a non-integer score. We can now use the familiar sort-and-list procedure to find the culprit:

```
> sort on diff, descending
> list case_id, score

case_id        score
5              82.3
1              78
2              91
4              84
3              77.8
```

The cases we want are listed at the beginning (positive differences) and end (negative differences) of the list. A better alternative, if our software allows it, is to list only the cases we're after:

```
> list case_id, score if diff ≠ 0
```

```
case_id        score
3              77.8
5              82.3
```

Impossibly missing value. The third kind of impossible value is a missing value in a variable that cannot have missing values. These will mostly be identification numbers and independent variables – any variable whose value we assign rather than measure. Every case must have a case id number; every patient in a drug study is either in the drug group or the placebo group; and so on. Suppose we have data from 50 patients. We can detect missing values by tabulating the variable:

```
> tabulate row=group
              freq.        %
drug          24           51.06
placebo       23           48.94
total         47           100.00
```

Cases with missing values of group are ignored, so the fact that only 47 patients are tabulated shows that there are three missing values. The sort-and-list method will find them because sorting does not ignore missing values; these are usually encoded as very big numbers and will appear first if we

```
> sort on group, descending
> list case_id, group

case_id        group
17             .
34             .
46             .
26             2
27             2
etc.
```

Again, if the sofware permits it we can, alternatively

```
> list case_id if group = .
case_id
17
34
46
```

Inconsistent values. So far we have made use of two kinds of context to spot errors: first, a distribution of values provides a context for identifying improbable values; second, the nature of each variable provides a context for identifying improbable and impossible values. Finally, each case itself provides a third kind of context: if two values within a case are inconsistent with one another, one or both may be wrong. A sample of mothers:

	case_id	age	#children	#boys	#girls
1	1	32	4	2	2
2	2	27	5	1	3
3	3	35	2	2	0
4	4	17	6	3	2
5	5	23	3	3	3

There's obviously an error in case 2: one boy and three girls doesn't add up to five kids. To find out which number is wrong we have to go back to the data sheet. Cases 4 and 5 have similar impossibilities. In addition, case 4 – a 17-year-old with six children – seems worth checking.

How do we find such errors? First, the impossible ones:

```
> create check, values = #boys + #girls
> create diff, values = #children - check
> compute mean of diff
```

If the mean isn't zero, there are errors; we can find them just as we did with the non-integer golf scores.

Second, the improbable ones:

```
> plot cases, x=age y=#children
```

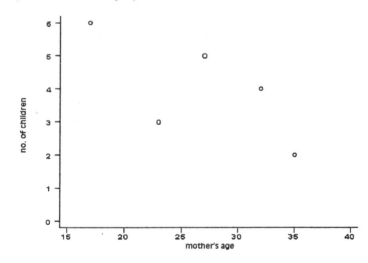

This scatterplot graphs each mother's number of children against her age. It is easy to see that there is one mother who is very young and has many children. What is her case number?

```
> plot cases, x=age y=#children symbol=case_id
```

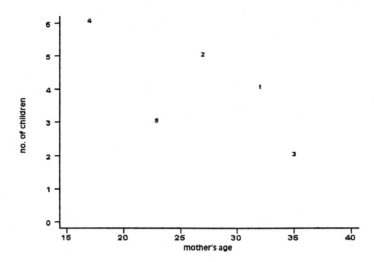

There she is in the upper left-hand corner: case number 4.

5.3   Exercises

1. Here are some housing sales data from the town of E. Westfield:

year	no. of sales	mean selling price ($1000)	mean days on market
1980	237	155	37
1981	241	170	-39
1982	254	16	34
1983	248	169	33
1984	276	183	29
1985	288	185	290
1986	2790	191	31
1987	301	188	22
1988	296	212	.19
1989	305	103	20
1990	289	210	20

Identify the improbable and impossible values.

2. Here are some batting data from the E. Westfield 1998 senior men's softball team:

name	pos.	at bats	1-base	2-base	3-base	hr	rbi	strikeouts	walks
Eddie	lf	105	18	3	0	2	12	4	3.2
Al	p	101	15	2	1	5	17	5	1
Jose	2b	99	21	5	4	12	39	2	5
Tom	rf	103	24	6	0	10	380	1	3
Dick	3b	18	18	4	4	10	36	4	4
Harry	1b	107	20	5	6.7	9	40	4	2
Irv	ss	103	200	7	4	10	38	3	3
Jack	cf	104	19	7	2	8	35	5	4
Walt	c	105	22	4	3	15	42	62	2

Identify the improbable and impossible values.

3. On the disk is a data set (crime.dat) containing information about every crime reported to the E. Westfield police in the years 1990 - 1999. The variables are as follows:

1	year	year of report
2	month	month of report
3	day	day of report
4	time	time of report (24-hr clock; e.g. 2:15 a.m. = 0215, 2:15 p.m. = 1415)
5	filenum	police file number
6	type	type of crime:

             1 = public nuisance
             2 = robbery
             3 = assault
             4 = rape
             5 = murder
             6 = theft
             7 = vandalism
             8 = fraud
             9 = other

7	arrests		number of arrests made
8	status	status of case:	1 = under active investigation

             2 = unsolved, inactive
             3 = investigation completed
             9 = other

For each variable, state the possible values or range(s) of values that variable may have in this data set. Then use your statistical software to find impossible or improbable values.

Demonstration 2

Looking at Faces, Part II

IN CHAPTER 3 we created a data set from a study of the relation between faces' perceived happiness and perceived attractiveness. Now we need to check those data and correct any errors we find.

```
> load file dennis1
```

We entered 80 subjects x 48 responses = 3840 observations - at least we think we did. This is easy to check:

```
> list variables
```

```
observations:      3,839
variables:         6
        1. subnum          subject number
        2. subsex          subject sex
        3. picnum          picture number
        4. picsex          picture sex
        5. group           group
        6. rating          rating (1=low, 7=high)
```

We seem to have left something out. If we can figure out what it is, we won't have to re-enter all the data. If there's one whole observation (i.e. every variable) missing, then one subject should be short one observation. We can use a one-way frequency table to see how often each subject appears in the data set:

```
> tabulate row=subnum
          subnum │  Freq.
     -------------------------
               1 │    48
               2 │    48
               3 │    48
               4 │    48
               5 │    47
               6 │    48
                 .
                 .
                 .
              80 │    48
     -------------------------
```

Now we know the missing observation belongs to subject 5, and we can also see that all the other subjects have the right number of observations (48). We'll look at the data to find out which of subject 5's responses didn't get entered:

	subnum	subsex	group	picnum	picsex	rating
213	5	2	1	21	1	5
214	5	2	1	22	2	5
215	5	2	1	23	1	3
216	5	2	1	25	2	3
217	5	2	1	26	1	5
218	5	2	1	27	2	3

The missing observation is subject 5's response to picture 24. We can fix this by inserting a new row and filling in the appropriate data:

	subnum	subsex	group	picnum	picsex	rating
213	5	2	1	21	1	5
214	5	2	1	22	2	5
215	5	2	1	23	1	3
216	5	2	1	24	2	2
217	5	2	1	25	2	3
218	5	2	1	26	1	5
219	5	2	1	27	2	3

Now we have the right number of observations overall, and the right number of observations for each subject, and no missing subject numbers. What about the other variables? Again some frequency tables will give us the answer:

```
> tabulate row=subsex
subject sex │   Freq.     Percent      Cum.
────────────┼──────────────────────────────────
     female │    1872       48.75     48.75
       male │    1968       51.25    100.00
────────────┼──────────────────────────────────
      Total │    3840      100.00
```

This table shows that there is the right number of values of subsex (3840), which means none are missing. Good. But 1872/48=39 female subjects, which is one too many, and 1968/48=41 male subjects, which is one too few; each group had 19 women and 21 men. This suggests that a male subject was mistakenly entered as a female subject. To find him, we can see which group has the wrong number of men:

```
> tabulate row=subsex, col=group
```

subject sex	group happy	attract.	Total
female	1008	863	1871
male	960	1008	1968
Total	1968	1871	3839

Right off the bat we can see trouble: the grand total is one short. We know there are no missing values of subsex, so this must reflect a missing value of group. As before, these frequencies are numbers of responses; there are 48 responses per subject, so if we divide each frequency by 48 we will convert it to a number of subjects:

subject sex	group happy	attract.	Total
female	21	17.979	38.979
male	20	21	41
Total	41	38.979	79.979

Now we can see that not only are there too many women, there are too many subjects in the happiness group as well. The fact that there are 48 (one subject's-worth) extra responses in the happiness group suggests that one subject in the attractiveness group was mis-entered as being in the happiness group. We are now looking for three things:

1) A subject, probably a female in the attractiveness group, missing one value of group.

2) A subject in the happiness group, listed as female, who is in fact male.

3) A female subject, listed in the happiness group, who is in fact in the attractiveness group.

Problem (1) we can fix as we did the missing observation, above. To solve problem (2) we need to compare each subject's sex as listed in the data set with that subject's response sheet.

```
> tabulate row=subnum, col=subsex
```

```
subject   subject sex
number  female     male   Total
----------------------------------------
     1      48        0      48
     2      48        0      48
     3       0       48      48
     4      48        0      48
     5       0       48      48
     6      48        0      48
     .
     .
     .
    80      48        0      48
----------------------------------------
 Total     1872     1968    3840
```

It turns out that subject 11 is the one we're looking for. While we're here, notice that this table confirms that every subject is consistently listed as male or female. Nobody has the right value of subsex for some observations and the wrong value for the rest.

We'll use the same strategy to fix problem (3):

```
> tabulate row=subnum, col=group
```

```
subject       subject sex
number     happy     attract.    Total
----------------------------------------
     1        48         0         48
     2        48         0         48
     .
     .
     .
    39        48         0         48
    40        48         0         48
    41         0        48         48
    42         0        48         48
     .
     .
     .
    62        48         0         48
    63        48         0         48
    64         0        48         48
     .
     .
     .
    80         0        48         48
----------------------------------------
 Total       1872      1968       3840
```

Subject 63 stands out clearly; we need to change group to 2 for all 48 of that subject's observations. That should take care of the subject variables. To be sure, we'll look at the same table that got us into this mess in the first place:

```
> tabulate row=subsex, col=group
subject │ group
sex     │  happy   attract. │ Total
────────┼──────────────────┼──────
 female │   912       912   │ 1824
   male │  1008      1008   │ 2016
────────┼──────────────────┼──────
  total │  1920      1920   │ 3840
```

Looks good. Now let's check the stimulus variables. Every subject saw the same pictures, so each picture number should occur 80 times in the data set:

```
> tabulate row=picnum
picture │
number  │ Freq.    Percent    Cum.
────────┼────────────────────────────
      1 │   80       2.08      2.08
      2 │   80       2.08      4.17
      3 │   80       2.08      6.25
      4 │   80       2.08      8.33
      5 │   80       2.08     10.42
      6 │   80       2.08     12.50
      · │
      · │
      · │
     48 │   80       2.08    100.00
────────┼────────────────────────────
  Total │ 3840      100.00
```

Good. We also know that there were 23 female faces and 25 male faces; therefore in 23 x 80 = 1840 observations picsex should be female (1) and in 25 x 80 = 2000 observations it should be male (2).

```
> tabulate row=picsex
picture │
sex     │ Freq.    Percent    Cum.
────────┼────────────────────────────
 female │ 1760      45.83     45.83
   male │ 2080      54.17    100.00
────────┼────────────────────────────
  Total │ 3840      100.00
```

The frequencies are off by exactly 80, suggesting that one of the pictures might have been entered with the wrong sex. We need to compare each picture's sex as listed in the data set with the correct value.

```
> tabulate row=picnum, col=picsex
```

picture number	picture sex female	male	Total
1	0	80	80
2	0	80	80
3	80	0	80
4	0	80	80
5	0	80	80
6	80	0	80
.			
.			
.			
48	0	80	80
Total	1760	2080	3840

It turns out that picture 26, entered as male, should be female. After fixing this the stimulus variables will be correct, and all that remains is to check the ratings.

```
> tabulate row=rating
```

rating (1-low, 7=high)	Freq.	Percent	Cum.
0	1	0.03	0.03
1	233	6.07	6.10
2	458	11.94	18.03
3	671	17.49	35.52
4	938	24.45	59.97
5	806	21.01	80.97
6	587	15.30	96.27
7	142	3.70	99.97
8	1	0.03	100.00
Total	3837	100.00	

This table shows two kinds of possible errors. First, there are only 3837 ratings, so three are missing. Unlike the other variables, rating can legitimately be missing (i.e. there was no response), but it is also possible that while entering the data we skipped a rating or two. Second, there are two ratings that have illegal values (0 and 8). Perhaps a subject found a face so attractive that a 7 couldn't do it justice, and perhaps we made a data entry error.

To check the missing ratings, we need to know which subjects and which pictures are missing ratings:

```
> list subnum picnum if rating==.
```

	subnum	picnum
1005	21	45
1650.	35	18
3455.	72	47

By referring to the response sheets, we can either confirm that these observations are missing a rating or find the ratings we missed and add them to the data set. To check the illegal ratings we follow the same strategy:

```
> list subnum picnum if rating==0
           subnum       picnum
   300.        7           12


> list subnum picnum if rating==8
           subnum       picnum
  2142.       45           30
```

Again we will refer to the response sheets to correct these values. If the illegal values represent data entry errors, we will correct them. If, on the other hand, the illegal values in the data set are in fact what the subject wrote, we will change them to missing because we don't know what they mean.

Transforming Data

Chapter Outline

1. Data analysis often requires making new variables or changing existing ones.
2. It is easy, and often necessary, to change string variables into numeric variables.
3. Continuous variables can be made discrete, but not vice versa.
4. Arithmetic operations on variables dramatically increase the scope of data analysis.

ARE RAW DATA like raw food? You can have your fish raw or cooked, and likewise your data, though you won't find recipes for cooking data in any textbook.[1] To cook data is to make them more to your liking, more consistent with your hypothesis. Cooking fish is cuisine, but cooking data is fraud.

Are raw data like raw materials? A factory takes in trainloads of ore, barrels of petroleum, bales of cotton, and turns out lawnmower blades, plastic dinosaurs, dental floss, and so on. A data analyst takes in raw data and produces ... what? Usually more questions, sometimes some conclusions. But just as General Motors does not directly transform iron ore into cars, a data analyst's conclusions are rarely based directly on raw data. In both cases it is usually necessary to turn the raw materials into something else before the final product can be produced. It is such intermediate transformations of the raw data – computed variables – that we are concerned with in this chapter.

One of the most common tasks in data analysis involves taking some of our data and transforming them in some way to make them useable for a specific purpose, like turning ore into sheet metal so we can make car bodies. These transformations fall into three broad categories: turning a string variable into a numeric variable, turning a continuous variable into a discrete one, and performing arithmetic operations on one or more variables.

---

[1] There are statistical manuals that are concerned solely with the practical and computational aspects of statistical tests; these books are often referred to, slightly pejoratively, as "cookbooks." The "cooking" going on here is not the transformation of raw into cooked but rather the following of a recipe.

6.1   Encoding string variables

Sometimes we have a data set that contains a string variable (one that contains a string of letters, such as a word, name, or code, instead of a number; see 3.3) that isn't doing us any good. For example:

party	income
"republican"	31000
"republican"	79000
"democrat"	28000
"republican	44000
"independent"	42000
"democrat"	62000
"democrat"	22000
...	...

The party name is in quotation marks to indicate that it is a string rather than a value label (see 3.5). If we try to get mean income by party

```
> compute mean of income, by party
```

we will get an error message. The problem here is that statistical software can't do much with a string variable. What it usually wants is a numeric variable, so what we have to do is to assign a unique numeric value to each different string; this process is known as *encoding*. When we say

the encoding process	

```
> encode party, newvar = partycode
```

we are telling the computer to do the following:

1. Examine the string variable and list the different strings occurring in it:

    republican
    democrat
    independent

2. Alphabetize the list and consecutively number the strings:

democrat	1
independent	2
republican	3

3. Create a new, numeric, variable and fill it with values according to the above correspondence. Thus for each case in which party = "democrat," partycode = 1, and so on.

Now the data set looks like this:

party	income	partycode
"republican"	31000	3
"republican"	79000	3
"democrat"	28000	1
"republican	44000	3
"independent"	42000	2
"democrat"	62000	1
"democrat"	22000	1
...	...	...

Our final step should be to label the values of partycode (see 3.5) so that our output will look right. Now we can get the means we wanted:

```
> compute mean of income, by partycode
partycode    |  mean of income
-------------+-----------------
democrat     |  37333.33
independent  |  42000.00
republican   |  51333.33
```

At this point you might be wondering why we went through all this rigmarole rather than making party a coded numeric variable from the start. Indeed, as we saw in Ch. 1, this is usually a reasonable thing to do. Nevertheless there are situations in which we wind up having to encode a string variable. One such situation is when the data were collected and entered by someone who didn't know that, by and large, categorical variables should be entered as codes rather than strings. Another situation is when we don't or can't know ahead of time what the values of a categorical variable will be, so we can't arrange a coding scheme before we enter the data. For example, we might ask people three questions:

Categorical variables should generally be entered as codes rather than strings.

1. What is your age?
2. What is your sex?
3. In one word, what is your major concern in life?

We are going to get many different responses to the third question. Some will be hard to anticipate and will be given by only a few respondents (e.g. "bowling," "apocalypse," "nitrites," etc.), but it is likely that there will be a few responses given by many respondents (e.g. "politics," "marriage," "football," "health," "children," etc.). We would like to know whether respondents' sex is associated with their major concerns. Our first impulse might be to use the same encoding procedure we used with the party/income data, and then tabulate sex by the encoded concern variable:

```
> encode concern, newvar = concerncode
> tabulate, row = concerncode col = sex
```

```
                    | sex
                    |
                    |
  concerncode       | female    male     total
  ------------------+----------------------------------
    aliens          | 1         0        1
    apocalypse      | 1         0        1
    bowling         | 0         1        1
    children        | 63        42       105
    communism       | 0         2        2
    crime           | 3         1        4
    football        | 1         37       38
    health          | 30        28       58
    marriage        | 40        40       80
    nitrites        | 2         0        2
    religion        | 45        40       85
    etc.
```

This might be ok, but if there are a lot of low-frequency responses the table will be bloated and hard to read. If we want to lump all the low-frequency responses into a single "other" category we need a more flexible way of encoding the concern variable. Let's break the operation down as we did earlier:

the "other" category

1. Examine the string variable and list the different strings occurring in it:

```
religion
crime
marriage
nitrites
etc...
```

2. Alphabetize the list. Consecutively number the high-frequency strings, and number all the low-frequency ("other") strings with a number that is greater than the highest code (the highest code is 5, so "other" will be 6):

```
aliens        6
apocalypse    6
bowling       6
children      1
communism     6
crime         6
football      2
health        3
marriage      4
nitrites      6
religion      5
```

3. Create a new, numeric, variable and fill it with values according to the above correspondence. For cases in which concern = "children," concerncode = 1, and so on.

Now, after labeling the values, we can make a more compact table:

```
> tabulate, row = concerncode col = sex
```

concerncode	sex female	male	total
children	63	42	105
football	1	37	38
health	30	28	58
marriage	40	40	80
religion	45	40	85
other	7	4	11

Notice that by giving "other" the highest code we make it come last in the list. This is where we want it because it does not represent any particular concern – it's not something we can interpret. This might tempt you to leave out the "other" category, but don't; we need it. Suppose our table looked like this:

concerncode	sex female	male	total
children	43	32	75
football	1	27	28
health	20	18	38
marriage	30	30	60
religion	35	30	65
other	57	54	111

This tells us that more than a quarter of our respondents reported concerns that were shared by few or no other respondents, which would weaken our claims about the prevalence of the first five concerns.

6.2   Making continuous variables discrete

Having investigated the association between concerns and sex, perhaps we want to know if people of different ages have different concerns. We might be tempted to ask for the mean age of people with each of the different concerns, but if there are many outliers – respondents who are much older or younger than most of the people listing a particular concern – then means may be misleading. It might be better to turn age into a categorical variable, where each category is a range of ages. This kind of age variable is undoubtedly familiar to you; here's how we make it.

Some statistical packages have commands that automate the process, but it is more instructive to do it manually. The first step is to create a new variable to contain the age category:

```
> create newvar agecat
```

The next step is to set all the values of the new variable to missing:

```
> let agecat = [missing]
```

This guarantees that any case that is not explicitly assigned a value for the new variable will have a missing value rather than an erroneous value. The last step is to group ages into age categories and assign the appropriate codes to all the cases:

```
> let agecat = 1 if age < 20
> let agecat = 2 if ((age ≥ 20) & (age < 30))
> let agecat = 3 if ((age ≥ 30) & (age < 40))
> let agecat = 4 if ((age ≥ 40) & (age < 50))
> let agecat = 5 if ((age ≥ 50) & (age <60))
> let agecat = 6 if age ≥ 60
```

Notice that there are no gaps or overlaps among the age categories defined by the above commands. Had we said

```
> let agecat = 1 if age < 20
> let agecat = 2 if ((age > 20) & (age <30))
```

then any case for which age = 20 would be unassigned, and would show up as missing (thanks to step two). On the other hand, had we said

```
> let agecat = 1 if age ≤ 20
> let agecat = 2 if ((age ≥ 20) & (age <30))
```

then any case for which age = 20 would first be assigned to agecat 1 and then to agecat 2. But which did we want? The command we used in the example

```
> let agecat = 2 if ((age ≥ 20) & (age <30))
```

avoids both kinds of ambiguity.

6.3   Arithmetic operations on one or more variables

Suppose we have a data set containing the year-end value and the net annual percentage gain of each stock (A and B) in our (small) stock portfolio:

year	A$	A_pct	B£	B_pct
1990	400.00	-15	200.00	+3
1991	360.00	-10	224.00	+12
1992	363.60	+1	228.48	+2
1993	403.60	+11	226.19	-1
1994	439.92	+9	235.24	+4
1995	457.52	+4	235.24	0

We probably have a number of questions about our stocks' performance. To begin with, what was the portfolio's average net gain each year? We can easily create a new variable containing the mean of the two stocks' net gains:

```
> create newvar avgnet
> let net = (A_pct + B_pct)/2
```

What was the largest percentage gain in a single stock in each year? To answer this we need to use a *function*, a procedure that performs a certain operation on one or more *arguments* and then returns a result. The function we need is one that returns the largest of two or more numbers; most programming languages and statistics packages have one.

```
> create newvar bigbucks
> let bigbucks = max(A_pct,B_pct)
```

The function max(A_pct,B_pct)simply returns the value of A_pct if it is greater than the value of B_pct, and returns the value of B_pct otherwise. Whichever value is returned becomes the value of bigbucks.

Finally, we might also want to know what our portfolio was worth at the end of each year. We could (and will) do this by adding together the values of stock A and stock B, but notice that A is valued in dollars and B is valued in pounds. To get the total value of our portfolio in dollars, we must first convert B from pounds to dollars. If the value of the pound against the dollar has been reasonably stable over the period in question, we might use an average exchange rate of, say, $1.70 to £1.00 to give us a rough measure of our portfolio's total value.

```
> create newvar B$
> let B$ = 1.7 * B£
> create newvar totval
> let totval = A$ + B$
```

(The asterisk (*) is widely used in computerland to indicate multiplication.) Now our data set contains answers to all the questions we have asked:

year	A$	A_pct	B£	B_pct	avgnet	maxgain	B$	totval
1995	400.00	-15	200.00	+3	-6	+3	340.00	740.00
1996	360.00	-10	224.00	+12	+1	+12	380.80	740.80
1997	363.60	+1	228.48	+2	+1.5	+2	388.42	752.02
1998	403.60	+11	226.19	-1	+5	+11	384.52	788.12
1999	439.92	+9	235.24	+4	+6.5	+9	399.91	839.83
2000	457.52	+4	235.24	0	+2	+4	399.91	857.43

We can do all kinds of things to our variables, far more than we can illustrate here. This example should, however, give you a sense of what is possible, of how easy it is, and of how it expands the scope of our analysis. When doing arithmetic on variables, be mindful of the order in which arithmetic operations are carried out ($\times$/+-), and be careful with (). For example, $3 + 4 \times 2 = 11$ but $(3 + 4) \times 2 = 14^2$. When talking to a computer it is important to say what you mean and to mean what you say.

6.4   Exercises

1. In the concerns study in 6.1, what would you do if you wanted the "other" response category to be listed first in the table?

2. The management at Crunchy Cracker Corp. distributes a questionnaire that includes the following question:

> How to you get to work?
>
> > 1) I drive my car.
> > 2) I take the subway.
> > 3) Other

Tallying the responses, they find:

---

[2] In the first case the multiplication is carried out first because of the order of operations, giving $4 \times 2 = 8$, then the addition, giving $3 + 8 = 11$. In the second case the addition is carried out first because it is in parentheses, giving $(3 + 4) = 7$, then the multiplication, giving $7 \times 2 = 14$.

```
trans. mode │  n
------------┼-----
drive car   │  47
take subway │  38
other       │ 139
```

What would you tell the Crunchy management about the design of this question? What would you recommend?

3. In the example in section 6.3, we assumed that the \$/£ exchange rate was more or less constant. This allowed us to use a single multiplier to convert pounds to dollars. What would you do if the rate was *not* constant?

4. Statistical software does not (yet) allow you to enter functions using mathematical notation because everything must appear on one line. For example instead of x^2, you have to say square(x). Instead of $\sqrt{x}$, you have to say sqrt(x). And instead of $\frac{x}{y}$ you would type x/y. Rewrite the following expressions for the computer.

a) $speed = \dfrac{distance}{time}$

b) $area = \pi\, r^2$

c) $y = ax^2 + bx + c$

d) $std.\ dev. = \sqrt{\dfrac{\sum (x - \bar{x})^2}{n}}$

6.5. Practice analysis: Who uses gloves?

The only thing I remember about my childhood dentist is his hairy knuckles. Now, in the AIDS era, health care workers are urged to wear gloves, regardless of how hairy their knuckles might be. It seems obvious that no one would want to take unnecessary risks with something like AIDS. But it takes some effort to convince young people to use condoms, and by the same token health care workers need to be educated about the importance of wearing gloves.

Friedland, Joffe, Moore, et al. (1992) evaluated the effectiveness of a glove-education program on all 23 nurses in the emergency department of a pediatric hospital. The nurses were observed, without their knowledge, before the program and one, two, and five months afterward. The observations were made during vascular access procedures (i.e. the patient was bleeding). For each procedure, the experimenters recorded whether the nurse wore gloves.

The variables in the data set are as follows:

1. Period:	Observation period
	1 = before intervention
	2 = one month after intervention
	3 = two months after
	4 = 5 months after intervention)
2. Observations:	Number of times the nurse was observed during that period
3. Gloves:	Number of times the nurse used gloves during that period
4. Experience:	Nurse's years of experience

Questions:

a. Is the data set organized casewise or scorewise?

b. What was the overall rate of glove use?

c. Make a graph showing the rate of glove use during each of the four observation periods.

d. Do you expect glove use to be higher among the more experienced nurses? Why or why not?

e. Separate the nurses into two experience categories: those with three years or less experience, and those with more than three years experience. Which group shows a higher rate of glove use?

f. Make a graph showing the rate of glove use in each period for each group of nurses.

g. Does three years seem an appropriate cut-off for dividing the nurses into less-experienced and more-experienced groups? Why or why not?

h. Do you think the answers to questions e and f would be different if you used a different cut-off? Why or why not? Try a cut-off of 8 years. What happens?

Data set:

P	O	G	E		P	O	G	E		P	O	G	E
1	2	1	15		3	2	1	9		1	1	0	14
2	7	6	15		4	.	.	9		2	.	.	14
3	1	1	15		1	2	0	15		3	.	.	14
4	.	.	15		2	3	2	15		4	1	1	14
1	2	1	2		3	1	1	15		1	.	.	14
2	6	5	2		4	2	1	15		2	2	2	14
3	11	10	2		1	6	1	8		3	3	3	14
4	9	9	2		2	1	1	8		4	1	1	14
1	5	5	3		3	2	2	8		1	.	.	8
2	13	13	3		4	.	.	8		2	1	1	8
3	8	7	3		1	3	0	8		3	1	1	8
4	15	14	3		2	4	3	8		4	1	1	8
1	2	0	10		3	8	6	8		1	.	.	3
2	2	2	10		4	2	0	8		2	2	1	3
3	2	2	10		1	2	0	2		3	.	.	3
4	5	4	10		2	3	3	2		4	.	.	3
1	12	0	20		3	8	8	2		1	.	.	6
2	2	2	20		4	5	5	2		2	1	1	6
3	3	3	20		1	1	0	5		3	.	.	6
4	3	0	20		2	.	.	5		4	.	.	6
1	3	0	8		3	.	.	5		1	.	.	3
2	8	8	8		4	.	.	5		2	1	1	3
3	3	2	8		1	1	0	15		3	.	.	3
4	4	2	8		2	3	3	15		4	.	.	3
1	4	4	9		3	.	.	15		1	.	.	1
2	4	4	9		4	.	.	15		2	.	.	1
3	.	.	9		1	1	1	3		3	2	2	1
4	.	.	9		2	2	2	3		4	.	.	1
1	4	0	9		3	1	1	3		1	.	.	6
2	4	4	9		4	1	1	3		2	.	.	6
										3	.	.	6
										4	1	0	6

(Note: . = missing)

6.6. Practice analysis: Evaluating reading instruction methods

Here is another data set containing before and after measures. In this case education researchers at Purdue University compared three methods of teaching reading (Baumann, Seifert-Kessell, & Jones, 1989). They randomly assigned each student to one of three teaching methods, and measured the student's reading comprehension before and after a period using that method. Two different reading comprehension measures were used in the pretest and three different comprehension measures were used in the posttest.

The variables in the data set are as follows:

1. Subject: Subject number
2. Group: Type of instruction (Basal, DRTA, or Strat)
3. PRE1:   Pretest score on first reading comprehension measure
4. PRE2:   Pretest score on second reading comprehension measure
5. POST1:   Posttest score on first reading comprehension measure
6. POST2:   Posttest score on second reading comprehension measure
7. POST3:   Posttest score on third reading comprehension measure

Questions:

a. Is this data set organized casewise or scorewise?

b. Do all of the test score variables seem to be normally distributed?

c. Should the three groups differ in the their pretest scores? Do they? Is this good news or bad news? Explain.

d. There are two ways to compare the three groups' reading improvement. One is to compare the three groups on each of the three posttest measures (i.e. one measure at a time). Another is to compare the three groups on the difference between the total of the posttest measures and the total of the pretest measures. What do you find using each method?

e. Which is the best instruction method? Make a bar graph showing the mean of the total posttest scores for each group. Now make a box plot showing the total posttest scores for each group. Which graph is more useful for analyzing data? Which is more useful for persuading people of something?

Data set:

S#	Group	Pr1	Pr2	Po1	Po2	Po3	S#	Group	Pr1	Pr2	Po1	Po2	Po3
1	Basal	4	3	5	4	41	34	DRTA	6	2	7	0	55
2	Basal	6	5	9	5	41	35	DRTA	8	4	10	6	57
3	Basal	9	4	5	3	43	36	DRTA	9	6	8	6	53
4	Basal	12	6	8	5	46	37	DRTA	9	4	8	7	37
5	Basal	16	5	10	9	46	38	DRTA	8	4	10	11	50
6	Basal	15	13	9	8	45	39	DRTA	9	5	12	6	54
7	Basal	14	8	12	5	45	40	DRTA	13	6	10	6	41
8	Basal	12	7	5	5	32	41	DRTA	10	2	11	6	49
9	Basal	12	3	8	7	33	42	DRTA	8	6	7	8	47
10	Basal	8	8	7	7	39	43	DRTA	8	5	8	8	49
11	Basal	13	7	12	4	42	44	DRTA	10	6	12	6	49
12	Basal	9	2	4	4	45	45	Strat	11	7	11	12	53
13	Basal	12	5	4	6	39	46	Strat	7	6	4	8	47
14	Basal	12	2	8	8	44	47	Strat	4	6	4	10	41
15	Basal	12	2	6	4	36	48	Strat	7	2	4	4	49
16	Basal	10	10	9	10	49	49	Strat	7	6	3	9	43
17	Basal	8	5	3	3	40	50	Strat	6	5	8	5	45
18	Basal	12	5	5	5	35	51	Strat	11	5	12	8	50
19	Basal	11	3	4	5	36	52	Strat	14	6	14	12	48
20	Basal	8	4	2	3	40	53	Strat	13	6	12	11	49
21	Basal	7	3	5	4	54	54	Strat	9	5	7	11	42
22	Basal	9	6	7	8	32	55	Strat	12	3	5	10	38
23	DRTA	7	2	7	6	31	56	Strat	13	9	9	9	42
24	DRTA	7	6	5	6	40	57	Strat	4	6	1	10	34
25	DRTA	12	4	13	3	48	58	Strat	13	8	13	1	48
26	DRTA	10	1	5	7	30	59	Strat	6	4	7	9	51
27	DRTA	16	8	14	7	42	60	Strat	12	3	5	13	33
28	DRTA	15	7	14	6	48	61	Strat	6	6	7	9	44
29	DRTA	9	6	10	9	49	62	Strat	11	4	11	7	48
30	DRTA	8	7	13	5	53	63	Strat	14	4	15	7	49
31	DRTA	13	7	12	7	48	64	Strat	8	2	9	5	33
32	DRTA	12	8	11	6	43	65	Strat	5	3	6	8	45
33	DRTA	7	6	8	5	55	66	Strat	8	3	4	6	42

Demonstration 3:

Comparing the nutritional content of breakfast cereals

EVERY MORNING MILLIONS of Americans stare glassy-eyed at millions of cereal boxes, and sometimes they wonder what their cereal is – or isn't – doing for them nutritionally. They turn to the little Federally mandated "Nutrition Facts" area on the side of the box and learn that each serving of Brand X provides 150 calories, 2 grams of fat, 3 grams of protein, 50% of their daily potassium needs, and so on. But is this good or bad? Is 2 grams of fat a lot or a little? Would they be better off eating Brand Y or Brand Z?

To answer questions like these we need data from all the cereal boxes we can find:

name	cal	pro	fat	sod	fib	crb	sug	pot	vit	shelf	wgt	vol
100% Bran	70	4	1	130	10	5	6	280	25	3	1	.33
100% Natural Bran	120	3	5	15	2	8	8	135	0	3	1	1
All-Bran	70	4	1	260	9	7	5	320	25	3	1	.33
All-Bran with Extra Fiber	50	4	0	140	14	8	0	330	25	3	1	.5
Almond Delight	110	2	2	200	1	14	8	-1	25	3	1	.75
Apple Cinnamon Cheerios	110	2	2	180	1.5	10.5	10	70	25	1	1	.75
Apple Jacks	110	2	0	125	1	11	14	30	25	2	1	1
Basic 4	130	3	2	210	2	18	8	100	25	3	1.33	.75
Bran Chex	90	2	1	200	4	15	6	125	25	1	1	.67
Bran Flakes	90	3	0	210	5	13	5	190	25	3	1	.67
etc.												

The variables are as follows:

name	name of cereal
cal	calories per serving
pro	protein (g) per serving
fat	fat (g) per serving
sod	sodium (mg) per serving
fib	dietary fiber (g) per serving
crb	complex carbohydrates (g) per serving
sug	sugars (g) per serving
pot	potassium (mg) per serving
vit	vitamins/minerals - typical % of rda
shelf	display shelf (counting from floor)
wgt	weight (oz.) of one serving
vol	volume (cups) of one serving

Our data set contains virtually all the information we might want to make a rational decision about what kind of breakfast cereal to eat. Some people may be most concerned with fiber, others with fat. Suppose we are concerned with calories. We could simply look through the data set, but there is an easier way. We can sort the data set so that the cereals are listed in order of increasing calories. Then all the low-calorie cereals will be at the top and all the high-calorie cereals will be at the bottom. But let's think before we compute. We're about to sort in order of calories per serving. We know what a calorie is, but what's a serving? Is it a standard unit (like a calorie)? Is a serving of Corn Flakes equivalent in some way to a serving of Grape Nuts? If we look at the data, we see that the answer is no. Some cereals' servings are bigger (in terms of weight and/or volume) than other cereals'.

The solution is to convert all the nutrient measures from the form nutrient-per-serving to the form nutrient-per-ounce or nutrient-per-cup.

```
> create newvar cals_per_ounce
> let cals_per_ounce = cal/wgt
```

Now we can sort the data set and make an ordered list:

```
> sort on cals_per_ounce, ascending
> output name, cals_per_ounce, calories
```

name	cals/oz.	cals/serving
1. All-Bran with Extra Fiber	50.0	50
2. All-Bran	70.0	70
3. 100% Bran	70.0	70
4. Raisin Squares	90.0	90
5. Bran Flakes	90.0	90
6. Shredded Wheat spoon size	90.0	90
7. Strawberry Fruit Wheats	90.0	90
8. Bran Chex	90.0	90
9. Nutri-grain Wheat	90.0	90
10. Shredded Wheat 'n'Bran	90.0	90
11. Raisin Bran	90.2	120
12. Fruitful Bran	90.2	120
13. Post Nat. Raisin Bran	90.2	120
14. Total Raisin Bran	93.3	140
15. Fruit & Fibre	96.0	120

etc.

Do we find the same cereals at the top of the list if we look at calories per cup?

```
> sort on cals_per_cup, ascending
> output name, cals_per_cup, calories
```

name	cals/cup	cals/serving
1. Puffed Rice	50.0	50
2. Puffed Wheat	50.0	50
3. Kix	73.3	110
4. Shredded Wheat	80.0	80
5. Honey-comb	82.7	110
6. Cheerios	88.0	110
7. Strawberry Fruit Wheats	90.0	90
8. Nutri-grain Wheat	90.0	90
9. Rice Chex	97.3	110
10. Wheaties	100.0	100
11. Cream of Wheat (Quick)	100.0	100
12. Maypo	100.0	100
13. Total Whole Grain	100.0	100
14. Product 19	100.0	100
15. Corn Flakes	100.0	100
.		
.		
.		
68. Raisin Nut Bran	200.0	100
69. Nutri-Grain Almond-Raisin	209.0	140
70. All-Bran	212.1	70

71.	100% Bran	212.1	70
72.	Cracklin'Oat Bran	220.0	110
73.	Clusters	220.0	110
74.	Mueslix Crispy Blend	238.8	160
75.	Oatmeal Raisin Crisp	260.0	130
76.	Great Grains Pecan	363.6	120
77.	Grape-Nuts	440.0	110

Which list is the one to use? It depends on whether you weigh your cereal or fill your bowl to some level. When we measure calories per ounce the fibrous, bran-y cereals look like the best bet, but when we measure calories per cup the same cereals are at the bottom of the heap, replaced by the more airy cereals. It is clear that the question "What is a serving?" does not have a simple answer.

recording an order in a variable

What if we would like to look at both orders at the same time? We can do this by using an ordered list to generate ranks. When we put data into a computer, the records are in some order, whether we have sorted them or not, and the computer refers to the first record in its memory as record 1. If we sort the records, then a different record becomes record 1. This internal variable – record number – is available to us, and we will use it to assign ranks.

First we sort on calories per ounce:

```
> sort on cals_per_ounce, ascending
```

Now we use the internal record number variable (recnum) to make a permanent record of the order that the records are currently in:

```
> create newvar cals_per_ounce_rank
> let cals_per_ounce_rank = recnum
```

Now we repeat the process for calories per cup:

```
> sort on cals_per_cup, ascending
> create newvar cals_per_cup_rank
> let cals_per_cup_rank = recnum
```

Now we can produce a list showing each cereal's rank in calories per ounce and in calories per cup. We might as well put them back in alphabetical order:

```
> sort on name, ascending
> output name cals_per_ounce, cals_per_ounce_rank, cals_per_cup,
  cals_per_cup_rank.
```

	name	cal/oz	rank	cal/cup	rank
1.	100% Bran	70.0	2	212.1	71
2.	100% Natural Bran	120.0	73	120.0	34
3.	All-Bran	70.0	3	212.1	70
4.	All-Bran with Extra Fiber	50.0	1	100.0	17
5.	Almond Delight	110.0	45	146.7	50
6.	Apple Cinnamon Cheerios	110.0	55	146.7	47
7.	Apple Jacks	110.0	53	110.0	20
8.	Basic 4	97.7	17	173.3	60
9.	Bran Chex	90.0	7	134.3	40
10.	Bran Flakes	90.0	4	134.3	38
	.				
	.				
	.				
68.	Special K	110.0	42	110.0	30
69.	Strawberry Fruit Wheats	90.0	9	90.0	8

70.	Total Corn Flakes	110.0	52	110.0	25
71	Total Raisin Bran	93.3	14	140.0	42
72.	Total Whole Grain	100.0	22	100.0	13
73.	Triples	110.0	49	146.7	46
74.	Trix	110.0	64	110.0	29
75.	Wheat Chex	100.0	36	149.3	52
76.	Wheaties	100.0	24	100.0	12
77.	Wheaties HoneyGold	110.0	68	146.7	43

The lists we have produced might be useful if the caloric value of cereals were the sole criterion for deciding what to eat for breakfast, but obviously it's not. A more sophisticated approach might be to decide which nutritional criteria we care about, and then to rank them. We could pick any number of criteria, but to keep things relatively simple let's pick three, and let's say they're fat, protein, and fiber, in that order.

sorting on more than one variable

Ranking our criteria this way has a specific meaning. Presumably we would like a cereal that is low in fat and high in protein and in fiber. There are three steps to finding one. First we sort our cereals on fat in an ascending order (low fat at the beginning of the list). Then we take all the cereals that have the same amount of fat and sort them in descending order on protein; in dataspeak we'd say "sort on protein within equal values of fat." Finally we sort on fiber within equal values of protein and fat, i.e. we take all the cereals that have the same amount of fat and protein and sort them in descending order on fiber. We can do all three steps with one command:

```
> sort on fat, ascending; on protein, descending; on fiber, descending
> output name fat protein fiber
```

	name	fat	protein	fiber
1.	Special K	0	6	1
2.	All-Bran with Extra Fiber	0	4	14
3.	Fruitful Bran	0	3	5
4.	Bran Flakes	0	3	5
5.	Shredded Wheat 'n'Bran	0	3	4
6.	Grape-Nuts	0	3	3
7.	Nutri-grain Wheat	0	3	3
8.	Shredded Wheat spoon size	0	3	3
9.	Frosted Mini-Wheats	0	3	3
10.	Product 19	0	3	1
11.	Cream of Wheat (Quick)	0	3	1
12.	Shredded Wheat	0	2	3
13.	Strawberry Fruit Wheats	0	2	3
14.	Raisin Squares	0	2	2
15.	Double Chex	0	2	1
16.	Crispix	0	2	1
17.	Corn Flakes	0	2	1
18.	Apple Jacks	0	2	1
19.	Puffed Wheat	0	2	1
20.	Golden Crisp	0	2	0
21.	Corn Chex	0	2	0
22.	Rice Krispies	0	2	0
23.	Corn Pops	0	1	1
24.	Frosted Flakes	0	1	1
25.	Honey-comb	0	1	0
26.	Puffed Rice	0	1	0
27.	Rice Chex	0	1	0
28.	100% Bran	1	4	10
29.	All-Bran	1	4	9
30.	Quaker Oat Squares	1	4	2
31.	Maypo	1	4	0

32. Post Nat. Raisin Bran	1	3	6
33. Raisin Bran	1	3	5
34. Total Raisin Bran	1	3	4
35. Total Whole Grain	1	3	3
36. Wheaties	1	3	3
37. Wheat Chex	1	3	3
38. Grape Nuts Flakes	1	3	3
39. Just Right Fruit & Nut	1	3	2
40. Honey Nut Cheerios	1	3	1.5
41. Bran Chex	1	2	4
42. Crispy Wheat & Raisins	1	2	2
43. Multi-Grain Cheerios	1	2	2
44. Wheaties Honey Gold	1	2	1
45. Smacks	1	2	1
46. Just Right Crunchy Nuggets	1	2	1
47. Froot Loops	1	2	1
48. Lucky Charms	1	2	0
49. Nut&Honey Crunch	1	2	0
50. Total Corn Flakes	1	2	0
51. Triples	1	2	0
52. Kix	1	2	0
53. Golden Grahams	1	1	0
54. Trix	1	1	0
55. Count Chocula	1	1	0
56. Cocoa Puffs	1	1	0
57. Fruity Pebbles	1	1	0
58. Cheerios	2	6	2
59. Quaker Oatmeal	2	5	2.7
60. Life	2	4	2
61. Fruit & Fibre	2	3	5
62. Nutri-Grain Almond-Raisin	2	3	3
63. Mueslix Crispy Blend	2	3	3
64. Raisin Nut Bran	2	3	2.5
65. Basic 4	2	3	2
66. Clusters	2	3	2
67. Oatmeal Raisin Crisp	2	3	1.5
68. Apple Cinnamon Cheerios	2	2	1.5
69. Almond Delight	2	2	1
70. Honey Graham Ohs	2	1	1
71. Cap'n Crunch	2	1	0
72. Muesli Raisins, Peaches, & Pecans	3	4	3
73. Muesli Raisins, Dates, & Almonds	3	4	3
74. Cracklin' Oat Bran	3	3	4
75. Great Grains Pecan	3	3	3
76. Cinnamon Toast Crunch	3	1	0
77. 100% Natural Bran	5	3	2

Demonstration 4

Effect of expectation on binocular fusion

IN DEMONSTRATION 3, our interest was in rearranging data to make them more useful; data manipulation was not only the means but the end. In the present case, on the other hand, our goal will be to test a hypothesis, and data manipulation will be a small but essential step in that direction.

One of the most important principles of cognitive psychology is the idea that what we perceive when we look at (or listen to) something is partly determined by what we expect to see (or hear). The present experiment is a very interesting demonstration of this principle.

The figure below is known as a random dot stereogram. A stereogram is a picture designed to be viewed through a stereoscope, a device that lets your left eye see only the left half of the stereogram and lets your right eye see only the right half. If you look at a stereogram of, say, the Taj Mahal through a stereoscope, it will seem to pop out at you in vivid 3D. If you look at the random dot stereogram below through a stereoscope you will see a diamond-shaped pattern seemingly floating above the background. The important difference between this and an ordinary stereogram is that it is impossible to know what you are going to see in a random dot stereogram until you look at it in the stereoscope — unless someone tells you.

<table>
<tr><td>a random dot stereogram</td></tr>
</table>

That's exactly what Frisby and Clatworthy (1975) did. When you look through a stereoscope you have to fuse two two-dimensional images into a single three-dimensional image, and this fusion process can take some time, particularly with random dot stereograms. If what we see is affected by what we expect to see, then showing subjects what they will see when they look in the stereoscope should reduce their fusion time.

In their experiment, Frisby and Clatworthy had two groups of subjects. Thirty-five subjects saw a drawing of what they would see when they had fused the two halves of the stereogram; the other group of 43 subjects did not see the drawing. All subjects then looked at the sterogram through a stereoscope and the experimenters measured the time it took each subject to fuse the images.

Here are the data (the fusion times are in seconds):

saw picture

19.70001	6.00000	2.40000
16.19998	5.90000	2.30000
15.90000	4.90000	2.00000
15.40002	4.60000	1.80000
9.70000	3.80000	1.70000
8.90000	3.60000	1.70000
8.60000	3.50000	1.60000
8.60000	3.30000	1.40000
7.40000	3.30000	1.20000
6.30000	2.90000	1.10000
6.10000	2.80000	1.00000
6.00000	2.70000	

didn't see picture

47.20001	8.90000	3.40000
21.99998	8.90000	3.10000
20.39999	8.40000	3.10000
19.70001	8.09999	2.70000
17.40000	7.90000	2.40000
14.70000	7.80000	2.30000
13.39999	6.90000	2.30000
13.00000	6.30000	2.10000
12.30000	6.10000	2.10000
12.20001	5.60000	2.00000
10.30000	4.70000	1.90000
9.70000	4.70000	1.70000
9.70000	4.30000	1.70000
9.50000	4.20000	
9.10000	3.90000	

A quick look at these data suggests that the picture group did indeed fuse the images faster than the no picture group. Let's see if we're right:

```
> compute mean of time, by group

group            N     mean   std dev
------------------------------------------
saw picture      35    5.55   4.80
no picture       43    8.56   8.08
```

The group means do show a difference in the predicted direction (picture group faster than no picture group) between the groups, but we need a statistical test to tell us whether this difference is reliable. Since we're asking a difference question and there are two groups (see the flow chart in Chapter 1) the appropriate test is a t-test for two independent samples. But look at the data again. The no-picture group's times seem to be not only longer (as predicted) but also more variable than the picture group's times, and the standard deviations above confirm this. Let's make a graph or two to get a better sense of how the times are distributed in the two groups before we do any tests.

A very direct way of graphing a distribution is the one-way scatterplot:

scatterplots of the
time variable

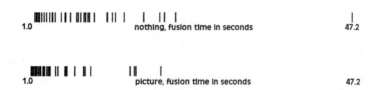

In this kind of graph each | represents one score (in this case, a fusion time). We can see three things here. First, the mean time is lower in the picture group. Second, the variability is greater in the no-picture group. Third, in both groups the distribution of times is quite positively skewed. We can see the same things in a different way in a box plot:

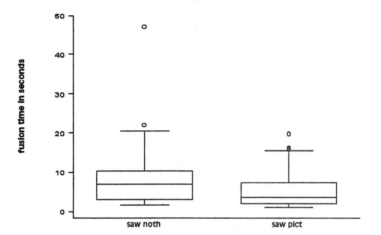

(The line through the middle of each box is the median; the bottom of the box is the 25th percentile and the top is the 75th percentile; the ends of the whiskers mark the upper and lower adjacent values. See 9.2 for details.) Again we can see what we saw in the scatterplots. First, the times are lower in the picture group (not only is the median lower, the whole box is lower). Second, the no-picture group's times are more variable (the interquartile range is bigger and the whiskers are longer). Third, the distribution of times in both groups is quite skewed (the upper whisker is longer than the lower whisker and, in the picture group, the 75th percentile is farther from the median than the median is from the 25th percentile).

The fact that we have unequal variances suggests that we should use the version of the t-test that does not assume equal variances. Unfortunately, we also have very skewed distributions, and all versions of the t-test assume normality. Are we stuck?

No. Situations like this arise quite often, and statisticians have developed a number of techniques for dealing with them. The basic idea is to transform the scores in a way that will change the shape of their distributions but will not alter the relative difference between groups. In this case, a likely solution is to take the log of the scores[3]:

---

[3] A thorough treatment of transformations is beyond the scope of this book. For the classic discussion of theory and practice, see Winer (1973).

```
> create newvar logtime
> let logtime = log(time)
```

Notice that we are applying the same transformation to both groups, and that the time scores themselves are not changed. Let's see if that did the trick.

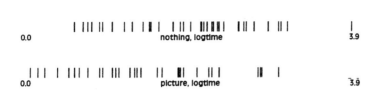

scatterplots of the transformed time variable

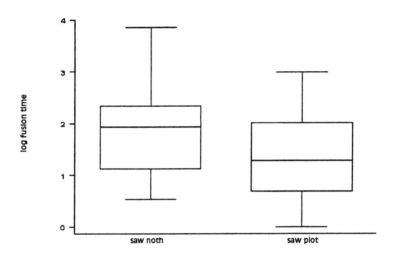

Both graphs show a big improvement: the log times are only a little skewed, and the variability of each group's scores is about the same[4]. Finally we have a variable that satisfies all the assumptions of the t-test.

```
> compute ttest: ind var = group, dep var = logtime, independent
  samples

group                  N      mean   std dev
--------------------------------------------
saw picture            35     1.39   0.82
no picture             43     1.82   0.81

degrees of freedom = 76
t = 2.3190
p (two-tailed) = 0.0231
```

---

[4] When you aren't sure and you need to be very careful, it is a good idea to test the equality of variance using, e.g., Bartlett's χ^2, and to test for normality using, e.g., the Shapiro-Wilk test.

Such a small probability value indicates that the difference between groups is quite unlikely to have occurred by chance, so we tentatively conclude that seeing the picture did indeed reduce subjects' fusion times.

Combining Data Sets

Chapter Outline

1. When two or more files contain data on the same variables we can append the files in order to work with all the data together.

2. When two or more files contain different variables of the same cases we can merge the files case by case in order to work with all the data together.

        a) 1-to-1 merge (all files have exactly the same cases)

        b) Match merge (all files have some cases in common)

S O FAR WE HAVE been talking about research situations in which we have all our data in one file. This is a reasonable way to begin, but often we have more than one file – sometimes many. In this chapter we will look at what to do when our data don't all come in one package.

7.1   Appending data

You and two collaborators have just conducted a rather large survey, and now you have 600 seven-page questionnaires to enter, no budget for clerical assistance, and an approaching deadline. What do you do? Pretty clearly a division of labor is the fair and efficient way to go. You could put the questionnaires in a box, toss in the code book and a floppy disk, and let one person enter the first 200 questionnaires, pass the box along to the next person, and so on. Fair, but not very efficient. A better strategy is to give each person 200 questionnaires, a copy of the code book, and a floppy disk, and then all work concurrently. It's fair and it's fast, but you'll wind up with data in three separate files.

No problem: you can *append* them to one another, just as you might tie a few short lengths of rope together to make a clothesline. In a little more detail, the whole process would go something like this:

> *Appending files joins them end to end.*

Step 1:   Create a code book (see 3.8).
Step 2:   Number the questionnaires (use any order, so long as each has a unique number).
Step 3:   Divide the questionnaires among the people who will be entering the data, and

give each a copy of the code book and a disk.

Step 4:   Enter the data, using the number on each questionnaire as the case_id number. It is essential that everyone enter their data in exactly the same way. It does not matter whether you make text files or native files, but everyone must use the same order of variables and the same format.

If you made native files in Step 4, go to Step 6.

Step 5a: If you made text files in Step 4, use a text editor to put the files together:
a. Open any of the files.
b. Go to the end of the file.
c. Insert another file.
d. Repeat b and c until done.
e. Save the whole thing; give the file an obvious name, e.g. *alldata.txt*.
f. Read the big text file into your statistics software and you're all set. Save it as a native file for future use.

Done.

Step 5b: Alternatively, read each text file into your statistics software and save it in native form; give each file a different name, e.g. *part1*, *part2*, etc.

Step 6:   If you made native files in Step 4 or in Step 5b, use your statistics software to put the files together:
a. Load the first native file (e.g. *part1*) into your statistics program.
b. Append the next file.
c. Repeat c until done.
d. Save the whole thing; give the file an obvious name such as *alldata*.

Done.

There's nothing much to the appending process. There are only two ways it can go wrong. First, you can inadvertently neglect to append one of the files, or you might append one of them twice. When you finish the appending process, check the number of cases in your data set. If it's too low, note which case numbers are missing and append the appropriate file; if it's too high, note which case numbers are duplicated and get rid of those cases.

Second, if you're not careful to use the same variable order in all files to be combined you'll have garbage rather than a data set. Here's what you want to avoid:

File 1:	X	Y	Z
	15	red	102
	14	blue	113
	17	blue	106
	etc.		

File 2:	X	Z	Y
	13	112	blue
	16	104	yellow
	15	109	red
	etc.		

All_data:	X	Y	Z
	15	red	102
	14	blue	113
	17	blue	106
	13	112	blue
	16	104	yellow
	15	109	red
	etc.		

The computer is not offended by this Frankensteinian data set, so it's your responsibility to avoid such monstrosities.

7.2   One-to-one merges

If appending data sets is like tying bits of string together to make something longer, merging data sets is like twisting several strings together to make a rope. When and why would we need to do this? Suppose we want to know how well high school gpa, SAT scores, and amount of financial aid predict college gpa. We identify a random sample of students, and from the admissions office we get:

last	first	hsgpa	SAT
Morgenstern	Eve	3.89	1490
Baker	Gloria	3.32	1330
Potter	Peter	3.20	1250
Horowitz	Holly	2.79	1040
Baker	Walter	2.41	970

From the financial aid office we get:

last	first	$
Baker	Walter	8065
Horowitz	Holly	6430
Baker	Gloria	6205
Potter	Peter	3960
Morgenstern	Eve	2580

From the registrar we get:

last	first	gpa
Baker	Gloria	3.41
Baker	Walter	3.09
Horowitz	Holly	2.82
Morgenstern	Eve	3.92
Potter	Peter	2.81

Now we put the data together. Strictly speaking we don't merge two files; rather, we merge the data in a file (the *file* data) with the data we're currently using (the *current* data). A one-to-one merge takes the first case of the file data and merges it with the first case of the current data, the second with the second, and so on. In carrying out this operation the computer does not care about the nature of the variables or the data sets involved.

```
> load file admissions
> sort on last first, ascending
> save file admissions
> load file fin_aid
> sort on last first, ascending
> save file fin_aid
> load file registrar
> sort on last first, ascending
> merge file admissions
> merge file fin_aid
```

last	first	cgpa	hsgpa	sat	fin_aid
Baker	Gloria	3.41	3.32	1330	6205
Baker	Walter	3.09	2.41	970	8065
Horowitz	Holly	2.82	2.79	1040	6430
Morgenstern	Eve	3.92	3.89	1490	2580
Potter	Peter	2.81	3.20	1250	3960

> *Merging files joins them side to side.*

When appending files we must make sure that both contain the same variables in the same variable order, and when merging we must make sure both files contain the same cases in the same case order. In the example we insured this by sorting each data set on the name variables. Had we not done this Gloria would have wound up with Eve's admissions values and Walter's financial aid value. Notice that although all files have the two name variables, these are not repeated when the three files are combined in one data set.

The program that does one-to-one merging mindlessly zips data sets together, first with first, second with second, until it runs out of material. This is all we need as long as the data sets to be merged are perfectly matched, as in the example, but in a less perfect world we need a slightly more sophisticated program.

7.3   Match merges

What if we don't have a value for every variable for every student in the sample? Suppose we get the following:

```
Admissions:      hs_gpa   sat      Financial Aid:        $
Baker      G     3.32     1330     Baker        G        6205
Baker      W     2.41     970      Horowitz     H        6430
Horowitz   H     2.79     1040     Morgenstern  E        2580
Potter     P     3.20     1250     Potter       P        3960
```

Both data sets have the same number of cases and both are sorted in the same order (i.e. by name), but a one-to-one merge will not work because the nth case (i.e. the first, second, etc.) in the three sets is not always the same person. This calls for a *match merge*: put cases together only if their case identifiers match, and leave missing values when no match is found.

Let's go through the match merge step by step. First we load one of the data sets; it doesn't matter which one.

```
> load file admissions
```

	last	first	hs_gpa	SAT	
1	Baker	Gloria	3.32	1330	
2	Baker	Walter	2.41	970	
3	Horowitz	Holly	2.79	1040	
4	Potter	Peter	3.20	1250	

```
> merge file fin_aid, match on last first
```

Merge looks at the current data and at the file data, finds that current case 1 and file case 1 match on the two match variables (last and first), and merges them. Next it looks at current case 2 and file case 2, and finds that they don't match. Current case 2 (Baker, W) comes before file case 2 (Horowitz, H), so the next case in the combined data set will be current case 2, with a missing value for the financial aid amount.

step	current	file	match?	source of hs_gpa & sat	source of fin. aid $
1	Baker,G	Baker,G	yes	current data	file data
2	Baker,W	Horowitz,H	no	current data	missing
3	Horowitz,H	Horowitz,H	yes	current data	file data
4	Potter,P	Morgenstern,E	no	missing	file data
5	Potter,P	Potter,P	yes	current data	file data

The important thing to notice here is what happens at step 2. Merge is not ready to put the file case (Horowitz) into the combined data set, and therefore merge does not go on to the next file case. In step 3 it is still trying to find a match for case 2 (Horowitz); it does, but this holding pattern could be maintained indefinitely, for as many current cases as precede file case 2. The same thing happens (in reverse) with the current case at step 4.

The current data set now consists of the merged admissions and financial aid data.

	last	first	hs_gpa	SAT	fin_aid
1	Baker	Gloria	3.32	1330	6205
2	Baker	Walter	2.41	970	.
3	Horowitz	Holly	2.79	1040	6430
4	Morgenstern	Eve	.	.	2580
5	Potter	Peter	3.20	1250	3960

Why didn't we include case id numbers in the data sets we just merged? Consider what would have happened. In the example, every variable was either a matching variable (one that occurs in both the current and file data) or a merging variable (one that occurs in only one of the data sets). The software combines (merges) the merging variables from the two data sets when it finds a pair of cases that match on the matching variable(s). Which type would case id be: merging or matching? If it appears in both sets, it can't be a merging variable; is it a matching variable? Let's try it with a simplified example:

> What happens to case id numbers in a match merge?

```
data set 1 (age):            data set 2 (sex):
case_id   name   age         case_id   name    sex
1         Anne   35          1         Anne    f
2         Bob    62          2         Chuck   m
3         Debby  51          3         Debby   f
```

Our problem is that between the two data sets there are four different names but only three different case id numbers. If we treat case_id as a matching variable

```
> load file age
> merge file sex, match on name case_id
```

the merge operation would proceed as follows:

			result	
step	current (age)	file (sex)	match?	age	sex
1	Anne, 1	Anne, 1	yes	35 (from current)	f (from file)
2	Bob, 2	Chuck, 2	no	62 (from current)	missing
3	Debby, 3	Chuck, 2	no	missing	m (from file)
4	Debby, 3	Debby, 3	yes	51 (from current)	f (from file)

The combined data set will look like this:

	case_id	name	age	sex
1	1	Anne	35	f
2	2	Bob	62	.
3	3	Chuck	.	m
4	4	Debby	51	f

The age and sex values are correct, but by including case_id as a matching variable we inadvertently gave Bob and Chuck the same id number.

If, on the other hand, we treat case_id as a merging variable

```
> merge file sex, match on name

ERROR:  duplicate variable names
```

the software balks because we are asking it to make a data set with two variables named case_id. The software will not allow this, and for good reason. In this case the two case_id variables would not only have the same name, but the same contents as well: a harmless duplication. But imagine two variables with the same name but different contents: how do we tell the software which one we mean? Your variables, like your children, should all have different names.

We are left with no choice but to leave the case_id variables out of the merge:

```
> delete case_id
> merge file sex, match on name
```

	name	age	sex
1	Anne	35	f
2	Bob	62	.
3	Chuck	.	m
4	Debby	51	f

The case_id variables have both been dropped. There was no point in making them in the first place. If we want our combined data set to have case id numbers, now is the time:

```
> sort on name, ascending
```
[this shouldn't be necessary after a merge, but it is good practice to sort whenever you're about to do something where order matters]

```
> create case_id, values = $row_num
```

The variable $row_num is a *system variable* (denoted by the $), i.e. one automatically created by the system. It is the number in the gray column at the left of the spreadsheet. Recall from 3.1 that it is not the same as a case id number, for row 1 is row 1 regardless of which case is in it.

	case_id	name	age	sex
1	1	Anne	35	f
2	2	Bob	62	.
3	3	Chuck	.	m
4	4	Debby	51	f

Now we're in business. This example demonstrates that in a merge operation there are in fact three types of variables: match variables, merge variables, and variables to be ignored (and therefore dropped). This is good, because sometimes (as in the example) we have identically named variables, and sometimes there are variables in one or both data sets which, though perfectly merge-able, we do not need in the combined data set.

What if there are identically named variables but we don't want to drop them? Suppose we have data sets containing the results of two horse races. Most but not all of the horses ran in both races, and we want to know how strongly correlated the horses' performances in the two races are. Here are the data sets:

```
     Kentucky Derby:                      Preakness:
horse           finish          horse            finish
Flicka          1               Trigger          1
Trigger         2               Black Beauty     2
Black Beauty    3               Flicka           3
Silver          4               Silver           4
Mister Ed       5               Tennessee Stud   5
```

We'd like a combined data set with horse's name, finish in the Kentucky Derby, and finish in the Preakness. The solution is simple:

```
> load file preakness
> rename variable finish = p_finish
> sort on horse, ascending
> save file preakness
> load file kderby
> rename variable finish = kd_finish
> sort on horse, ascending
> merge file preakness, match on horse
```

	horse	kd_finish	p_finish
1	Black Beauty	3	2
2	Flicka	1	3
3	Mister Ed	5	.
4	Silver	4	4
5	Tennessee Stud	.	5
6	Trigger	2	1

Now we can compute the correlation we wanted:

```
> compute correlation of kd_finish p_finish
n = 4  r = 0.40
```

Note that n (the number of pairs of scores) is four because two horses have a missing score and cannot be included in the computation.

7.4   Summary

Until you've had a little practice merging and appending, it can be hard to figure out when to do which. Here are some guidelines that should help when you have two data sets to combine:

Situation	Operation	Notes
Both data sets contain the same variables and different cases	append	variables must be in same order
Both data sets contain exactly the same cases and at least some different variables	one-to-one merge	cases must be in same order
Both data sets contain at least some of the same cases and have at least one case identifying variable in common	match merge	cases must be in same order
The data sets contain none of the same cases but have at least one variable in common	delete non-shared variables and append what remains	remaining variables must be in same order
The data sets contain none of the same cases and have no variable in common	sets cannot be combined	

These guidelines apply whether you have two data sets or dozens, because you combine two at a time.

7.5   Exercises

1. In the example in 7.3, suppose a third data set is obtained from the registrar containing students' current grade point averages:

```
                      gpa
    Baker      G      3.41
    Baker      W      3.09
    Horowitz   H      2.82
    Morgenstern E     3.92
```

Merge this set with the other two and list the resulting data set.

2. The Yankees were the champions of the 1998 baseball season, but the heroes were Mark McGwire and Sammy Sosa, who both broke a record that had stood for 37 years. In 1961 Roger Maris hit 61 home runs for the Yankees, breaking the record of 60 set by Babe Ruth, also for the Yankees, in 1927. In September of 1998 McGwire hit his 62nd season home run, and Sosa did the same five days later. McGwire finished the season with 70 home runs, Sosa with 66.

Watching one player creeping up on and passing Maris's record would have been thrilling enough for baseball fans, but watching two players racing to beat the record was one of the most exciting things to happen in baseball in decades. If we want to reconstruct this race and to understand a little better the circumstances of this extraordinary contest, we can easily get the necessary data. For this exercise we have two data sets, one describing McGwire's and one describing Sosa's 1998 season (Simonoff, 1998). Both data sets contain the same variables:

Cardinals	Cubs
Game number	Game number
Days since beginning of season	Days since beginning of season
Game location (0=away, 1=home)	Game location (0 = away, 1 = home)
Runs scored by Cardinals	Runs scored by Cubs
Runs scored by opposition	Runs scored by opposition
Number of home runs hit by McGwire	Number of home runs hit by Sosa
Runs driven in by McGwire's home runs	Runs driven in by Sosa's home runs
McGwire game status	Sosa game status
(0=played, 1=didn't play)	(0=played, 1=didn't play)

Both data sets are supplied as text files: homerun1.txt and homerun2.txt.

a. Read the Cardinals data into your statistics program. Name and label the variables, and label values where appropriate. Save the data as a native file. Do the same for the Cubs data.

b. For each team, create a new variable indicating whether the team won or lost. Use an if operation (see chapter 4) to determine the values of this variable.

c. Combine the two data sets in the way that will permit you to create a graph that will show which of the two sluggers was ahead at each game number.

d. In Ruth's day the baseball season was 154 games long; by 1961 it had been lengthened to 162 games. The baseball commissioner ruled that because Maris had played in a longer season, Ruth's record would stand until broken within 154 games (Maris had 59 home runs in

154 games). Did McGwire and Sosa meet this requirement?

e. What proportion of their home and away games did the Cardinals and the Cubs win?

f. Did Sosa and McGwire hit more home runs in home games than in away games?

g. Were the Cardinals more likely to win when McGwire was playing? Were the Cubs more likely to win when Sosa was playing?

Demonstration 5

GNP and Life Expectancy

POVERTY IS THE RELATIVE LACK of money, but looking at income or wealth is not the only way to measure poverty. Poverty expresses itself in many ways, such as low literacy rates and poor nutrition. We have two data sets, each of which contains some of these aspects of poverty. Set 1 (Rouncefield, 1995) contains observations on 6 variables for 97 countries:

country	[Country name]
birth	[Live birth rate per 1,000 of population]
death	[Death rate per 1,000 of population]
infdeath	[Infant deaths per 1,000 of population under 1 year old]
lifexp_m	[Life expectancy at birth for males]
lifexp_f	[Life expectancy at birth for females]
gnp_pc	[Gross National Product per capita in U.S. dollars]

Set 2 (Rossman, 1994) contains observations on 5 variables for the 40 largest countries:

country	[Country name]
lifexp	[Life expectancy]
pptv	[People per television]
ppp	[People per physician]
lifexp_f	[Female life expectancy]
lifexp_m	[Male life expectancy]

Combining the two would give us a single data set with an interesting collection of variables:

country	[Country]
birth	[Live birth rate per 1,000 of population]
death	[Death rate per 1,000 of population]
infdeath	[Infant deaths per 1,000 of population under 1 year old]
lifexp_m	[Life expectancy at birth for males]
lifexp_f	[Life expectancy at birth for females]
lifexp	[Average life expectancy]
pptv	[People per television]
ppp	[People per physician]
gnp_pc	[Gross National Product per capita in U.S. dollars]

Data set 2's male and female life expectancy variables are already in set 1, but set 2 adds average life expectancy, as well as people per television and per physician.

What sort of operation are we looking for? Referring to the guidelines in 7.4, we see that both data sets contain at least some of the same cases (countries) and have at least one case identifying variable in common (country name). Therefore a match merge is appropriate.

The next question is: What is our matching variable? We know that it must be a case identifying variable that the two data sets have in common. Although these two data sets have several variables in common, only country is a case identifying variable; it is sure to have a unique value for each case. (Two countries might have the same female life expectancy, but they can't have the same name.) Therefore country will be our matching variable. Because our matching variable has strings as values, we need to make sure that values in the two data sets that should match will match.

```
> load file set1
> sort on country, ascending
> list country
```

1.	Afghanistan	34.	Guyana	67.	Poland
2.	Albania	35.	Hong_Kong	68.	Portugal
3.	Algeria	36.	Hungary	69.	Romania
4.	Angola	37.	India	70.	Saudi_Arabia
5.	Argentina	38.	Indonesia	71.	Sierra_Leone
6.	Austria	39.	Iran	72.	Singapore
7.	Bahrain	40.	Iraq	73.	Somalia
8.	Bangladesh	41.	Ireland	74.	South_Africa
9.	Belgium	42.	Israel	75.	Spain
10.	Bolivia	43.	Italy	76.	Sri_Lanka
11.	Botswana	44.	Japan	77.	Sudan
12.	Brazil	45.	Jordan	78.	Swaziland
13.	Bulgaria	46.	Kenya	79.	Sweden
14.	Byelorussian_SSR	47.	Korea	80.	Switzerland
15.	Cambodia	48.	Kuwait	81.	Tanzania
16.	Canada	49.	Lebanon	82.	Thailand
17.	Chile	50.	Libya	83.	Tunisia
18.	China	51.	Malawi	84.	Turkey
19.	Columbia	52.	Malaysia	85.	U.K.
20.	Congo	53.	Mexico	86.	U.S.A.
21.	Czechoslovakia	54.	Mongolia	87.	USSR
22.	Denmark	55.	Morocco	88.	Uganda
23.	Ecuador	56.	Mozambique	89.	Ukrainian_SSR
24.	Egypt	57.	Namibia	90.	United_Arab_Emirates
25.	Ethiopia	58.	Nepal	91.	Uruguay
26.	Finland	59.	Netherlands	92.	Venezuela
27.	Former_E._Germany	60.	Nigeria	93.	Vietnam
28.	France	61.	Norway	94.	Yugoslavia
29.	Gabon	62.	Oman	95.	Zaire
30.	Gambia	63.	Pakistan	96.	Zambia
31.	Germany	64.	Paraguay	97.	Zimbabwe
32.	Ghana	65.	Peru		
33.	Greece	66.	Philippines		

```
> load file set2
> sort on country, ascending
> list country
```

1.	Argentina	15.	Japan	29.	Spain
2.	Bangladesh	16.	Kenya	30.	Sudan
3.	Brazil	17.	Korea, North	31.	Taiwan
4.	Canada	18.	Korea, South	32.	Tanzania
5.	China	19.	Mexico	33.	Thailand
6.	Colombia	20.	Morocco	34.	Turkey
7.	Egypt	21.	Myanmar (Burma)	35.	Ukraine
8.	Ethiopia	22.	Pakistan	36.	United Kingdom
9.	France	23.	Peru	37.	United States
10.	Germany	24.	Philippines	38.	Venezuela
11.	India	25.	Poland	39.	Vietnam
12.	Indonesia	26.	Romania	40.	Zaire
13.	Iran	27.	Russia		
14.	Italy	28.	South Africa		

The first case that appears in both sets is Argentina, and this case has the same identifier in both sets: "Argentina" will match "Argentina." Fine. But scanning the lists we can see that there are a few cases that will not match, mostly in the Us. We know that "U.K." should match "United Kingdom," but the computer doesn't, so we must change one – it doesn't matter which – to match the other. We find the same problem in the case of the U.S. and Ukraine, and we must fix these too.

Sometimes there is no fix. Set 1 has "Korea" and set 2 has "Korea, North" and "Korea, South." Which Korea is in set 1? Unless we can find out, there will be no match.

Once we have fixed the country names, we are ready to merge. As we saw in Chapter 7, to merge files we must first sort both files in the same order on the matching variable:

```
> load file set1
> sort on country, ascending
> save file set1
> load file set2
> sort on country, ascending
> save file set2
```

Now we can load one file into memory and then merge the other:

```
> load file set1
> merge file set2, match on country
```

After a merge, it's a good idea to look at the data to make sure we got what we wanted:

```
> list
```

country	gnp_pc	birth	death	inf_dth	le_m	le_f	av_le	pptv	ppp
Afghanistan	168	40.4	18.7	181.6	41	42	.	.	.
Albania	600	24.7	5.7	30.8	69.6	75.5	.	.	.
Algeria	2060	35.5	8.3	74	61.6	63.3	.	.	.
Angola	610	47.2	20.2	137	42.9	46.1	.	.	.
Argentina	2370	20.7	8.4	25.7	65.5	72.7	70.5	4	370
Austria	17000	14.9	7.4	8	73.3	79.6	.	.	.
Bahrain	6340	28.4	3.8	16	66.8	69.4	.	.	.
Bangladesh	210	42.2	15.5	119	56.9	56	53.5	315	6166
Belgium	15540	12	10.6	7.9	70	76.8	.	.	.
Bolivia	630	46.6	18	111	51	55.4	.	.	.
Botswana	2040	48.5	11.6	67	52.3	59.7	.	.	.
Brazil	2680	28.6	7.9	63	62.3	67.6	65	4	684
Bulgaria	2250	12.5	11.9	14.4	68.3	74.7	.	.	.
Byelorussian_SSR	1880	15.2	9.5	13.1	66.4	75.9	.	.	.

Cambodia	.	41.4	16.6	130	47	49.9	.	.	.
Canada	20470	14.5	7.3	7.2	73	79.8	76.5	1.7	449
Chile	1940	23.4	5.8	17.1	68.1	75.1	.	.	.
China	380	21.2	6.7	32	68	70.9	70	8	643
Colombia	1260	27.4	6.1	40	63.4	69.2	71	5.6	1551
Congo	1010	46.1	14.6	73	50.1	55.3	.	.	.
Czechoslovakia	2980	13.4	11.7	11.3	71.8	77.7	.	.	.
Denmark	22080	12.4	11.9	7.5	71.8	77.7	.	.	.
Ecuador	980	32.9	7.4	63	63.4	67.6	.	.	.
Egypt	600	38.8	9.5	49.4	57.8	60.3	60.5	15	616
Ethiopia	120	48.6	20.7	137	42.4	45.6	51.5	503	36660
Finland	26040	13.2	10.1	5.8	70.7	78.7	.	.	.
Former_E_ Germany	.	12	12.4	7.6	69.8	75.9	.	.	.
France	19490	13.6	9.4	7.4	72.3	80.5	78	2.6	403
Gabon	390	39.4	16.8	103	49.9	53.2	.	.	.
Gambia	260	47.4	21.4	143	41.4	44.6	.	.	.
Germany	22320	11.4	11.2	7.4	71.8	78.4	76	2.6	346
Ghana	390	44.4	13.1	90	52.2	55.8	.	.	.
Greece	5990	10.1	9.2	11	65.4	74	.	.	.
Guyana	330	28.3	7.3	56	60.4	66.1	.	.	.
Hong_Kong	14210	11.7	4.9	6.1	74.3	80.1	.	.	.
Hungary	2780	11.6	13.4	14.8	65.4	73.8	.	.	.
India	350	30.5	10.2	91	52.5	52.1	57.5	44	2471
Indonesia	570	28.6	9.4	75	58.5	62	61	24	7427
Iran	2490	42.5	11.5	108.1	55.8	55	64.5	23	2992
Iraq	3020	42.6	7.8	69	63	64.8	.	.	.
Ireland	9550	15.1	9.1	7.5	71	76.7	.	.	.
Israel	10920	22.3	6.3	9.7	73.9	77.4	.	.	.
Italy	16830	9.7	9.1	8.8	72	78.6	78.5	3.8	233
Japan	25430	9.9	6.7	4.5	75.9	81.8	79	1.8	609
Jordan	1240	38.9	6.4	44	64.2	67.8	.	.	.
Kenya	370	47	11.3	72	56.5	60.5	61	96	7615
Korea	.	23.5	18.1	25	66.2	72.7	.	.	.
Korea, North	.	.	.	.	67	73	70	90	370
Korea, South	.	.	.	.	67	73	70	4.9	1066
Kuwait	16150	26.8	2.2	15.6	71.2	75.4	.	.	.
Lebanon	.	31.7	8.7	48	63.1	67	.	.	.
Libya	5310	44	9.4	82	59.1	62.6	.	.	.
Malawi	200	48.3	25	130	38.1	41.2	.	.	.
Malaysia	2320	31.6	5.6	24	67.5	71.6	.	.	.
Mexico	2490	29	23.2	43	62.1	66	72	6.6	600
Mongolia	110	36.1	8.8	68	60	62.5	.	.	.
Morocco	960	35.5	9.8	82	59.1	62.5	64.5	21	4873
Mozambique	80	45	18.5	141	44.9	48.1	.	.	.
Myanmar (Burma)	.	.	.	.	53	56	54.5	592	3485
Namibia	1030	44	12.1	135	55	57.5	.	.	.
Nepal	170	39.6	14.8	128	50.9	48.1	.	.	.
Netherlands	17320	13.2	8.6	7.1	73.3	79.9	.	.	.
Nigeria	360	48.5	15.6	105	48.8	52.2	.	.	.
Norway	23120	14.3	10.7	7.8	67.2	75.7	.	.	.
Oman	5220	45.6	7.8	40	62.2	65.8	.	.	.
Pakistan	380	30.3	8.1	107.7	59	59.2	56.5	73	2364
Paraguay	1110	34.8	6.6	42	64.4	68.5	.	.	.
Peru	1160	32.9	8.3	109.9	56.8	66.5	64.5	14	1016
Philippines	730	33.2	7.7	45	62.5	66.1	64.5	8.8	1062
Poland	1690	14.3	10.2	16	67.2	75.7	73	3.9	480

	gnp_pc	birth	death	infdeath	lifexp_m	lifexp_f	lifexp	pptv	ppp
Portugal	7600	11.9	9.5	13.1	66.5	72.4	.	.	.
Romania	1640	13.6	10.7	26.9	66.5	72.4	72	6	559
Russia	2242	17.7	10	23	64.6	74	69	3.2	259
Saudi_Arabia	7050	42.1	7.6	71	61.7	65.2	.	.	.
Sierra_Leone	240	48.2	23.4	154	39.4	42.6	.	.	.
Singapore	11160	17.8	5.2	7.5	68.7	74	.	.	.
Somalia	120	50.1	20.2	132	43.4	46.6	.	.	.
South Africa	2530	32.1	9.9	72	57.5	63.5	64	11	1340
Spain	11020	10.7	8.2	8.1	72.5	78.6	78.5	2.6	275
Sri_Lanka	470	21.3	6.2	19.4	67.8	71.7	.	.	.
Sudan	480	44.6	15.8	108	48.6	51	53	23	12550
Swaziland	810	46.8	12.5	118	42.9	49.5	.	.	.
Sweden	23660	14.5	11.1	5.6	74.2	80	.	.	.
Switzerland	34064	12.5	9.5	7.1	73.9	80.	.	.	.
Taiwan	.	.	.	.	72	78	75	3.2	965
Tanzania	110	50.5	14	106	51.3	54.7	52.5	.	25229
Thailand	1420	22.3	7.7	28	63.8	68.9	68.5	11	4883
Tunisia	1440	31.1	7.3	52	64.9	66.4	.	.	.
Turkey	1630	29.2	8.4	76	62.5	65.8	70	5	1189
Uganda	220	52.2	15.6	103	49.9	52.7	.	.	.
Ukraine	1320	13.4	11.6	13	66.4	74.8	70.5	3	226
United Kingdom	16100	13.6	11.5	8.4	72.2	77.9	76	3	611
United States	21790	16.7	8.1	9.1	71.5	78.3	75.5	1.3	404
United_Arab_Emirates	19860	22.8	3.8	26	68.6	72.9	.	.	.
Uruguay	2560	18	9.6	21.9	68.4	74.9	.	.	.
Venezuela	2560	27.5	4.4	23.3	66.7	72.8	74.5	5.6	576
Vietnam	.	31.8	9.5	64	63.7	67.9	65	29	3096
Yugoslavia	.	14	9	20.2	68.6	74.5	.	.	.
Zaire	220	45.6	14.2	83	50.3	53.7	54	.	23193
Zambia	420	51.1	13.7	80	50.4	52.5	.	.	.
Zimbabwe	640	41.7	10.3	66	56.5	60.1	.	.	.

Set 1 had 97 cases and set 2 had 40 cases; the data set created by merging the two has 101 cases. 101 minus 97 equals four countries (N. Korea, S. Korea, Myanmar, and Taiwan) in set 2 that were not in set 1. Conversely, 101 minus 40 equals 61 countries in set 1 that were not in set 2. This leaves 36 countries that were in both sets.

Those 36 countries will allow us to look at the relations between variables from set 1 and variables from set 2. One way to quickly describe the relations among several quantitative variables is to ask for a *correlation matrix*:

```
> compute correlation of gnp_pc birth death infdeath lifexp_m lifexp_f lifexp pptv ppp
```

	gnp_pc	birth	death	infdeath	lifexp_m	lifexp_f	lifexp	pptv
gnp_pc	1.0000							
birth	-0.6291	1.0000						
death	-0.3028	0.4862	1.0000					
infdeath	0.6016	0.8584	0.6546	1.0000				
lifexp_m	0.6430	-0.8665	-0.7335	-0.9368	1.0000			
lifexp_f	0.6500	-0.8944	-0.6930	-0.9554	0.9830	1.0000		
lifexp	0.6921	-0.8910	-0.4571	-0.9001	0.9422	0.9486	1.0000	
pptv	-0.2397	0.5335	0.5642	0.5924	-0.5649	-0.5579	-0.6058	1.0000
ppp	-0.3052	0.6672	0.5835	0.6091	-0.7127	-0.6697	-0.6660	0.6197

The matrix contains the correlation coefficient for every pair of variables. The first cell contains the correlation between gnp_pc and gnp_pc, which, not surprisingly, is 1[1]. The cell below this contains the correlation between gnp_pc and birth (-0.6291); and so on. There are many things to explore here. By way of illustration, let's focus on the relations between per capita gnp and some of the other variables. GNP seems to be positively correlated with life expectancy. It's no surprise that people in more affluent countries live longer, but a correlation coefficient doesn't necessarily tell the whole story. We should look at a scatterplot:

```
> plot cases, x=gnp_pc, y=lifexp
```

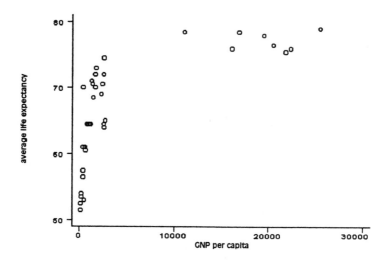

Remember that the correlation coefficient measures the strength of the linear relation between two variables. There's a relation here, but it doesn't look very linear. The countries clustered at the left of the graph don't vary much in per capita GNP but vary enormously in life expectancy. The countries clustered at the top of the graph, conversely, vary considerably in per capita GNP but don't vary much in life expectancy. One approach to a situation like this, where the cases cluster in two widely separated groups is to ask who's who. Would the graph make more sense if we knew which country a given dot represented?

```
> plot cases, x=gnp_pc, y=lifexp, symbol=country
```

---

[1] It is not obvious to me why, but this piece of non-information seems to be a general feature of correlation maxtrixes. Ignore it.

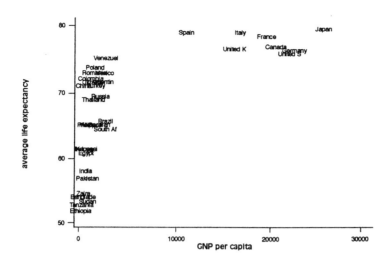

The identity of the eight countries with the highest life expectancies and the highest per capita GNPs is not surprising. The graph is split roughly into the so-called industrialized and developing nations. Suppose we treat them separately:

```
> create group, values = .
> change group = 1 if gnp_pc < 10000
> change group = 2 if gnp_pc > 10000
> plot cases if group = 1, x=gnp_pc, y=lifexp, symbol=country
```

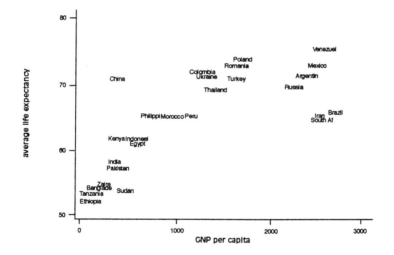

Now we see that there is in fact a fairly strong relation between per capita GNP and life expectancy in the developing nations, and it is approximately linear; we couldn't see it in the first graph because the x-axis there had to accommodate a much larger range of GNP values. We can also calculate the correlation coefficient separately for this group:

```
> compute correlation of lifexp gnp_pc if group = 1
r = 0.7182
```

Let's do the same with the other group:

```
>plot cases if group = 2, x=gnp_pc, y=lifexp, symbol=country
```

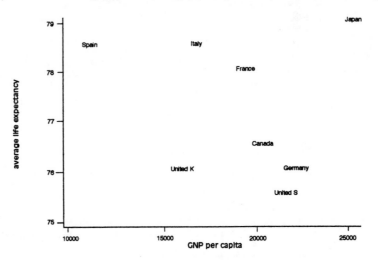

```
> compute correlation of lifexp gnp_pc if group = 2
  r = -0.1749
```

Among the industrialized nations, there is not any obvious relation between per capita GNP and life expectancy, primarily because life expectancy is fairly uniformly high in all of them (notice the small range of values on the y-axis).

Demonstration 6

Popularity and Priorities

CHASE AND DUMMER (1992) asked children the following questions:

Which of the following would make you popular among your friends? Rank in order.
- A. Make good grades.
- B. Having lots of money.
- C. Being good at sports.
- D. Being handsome or pretty.

What is most important to you?
- A. To make good grades.
- B. To be popular.
- C. To be good in sports.

The children were 478 students in grades 4-6 from three school districts in Michigan. One district was urban, one suburban, and one rural; roughly a third of the sample came from each district. Here are the variables and their values:

1. Gender	boy or girl	
2. Grade	4, 5 or 6	
3. Age	age in years	
4. Race	white, other	
5. District	rural, suburban, or urban school district	
6. School	name of school	
7. Goals	student's choice in the personal goals question where options were 1 = make good grades, 2 = be popular, 3 = be good in sports	
8. Grades	rank of "make good grades" (1=most important for popularity, 4=least important)	
9. Sports	rank of "being good at sports" (1=most important for popularity, 4=least important)	
10. Looks	rank of "being handsome or pretty" (1=most important for popularity, 4=least important)	
11. Money	rank of "having lots of money" (1=most important for popularity, 4=least important)	

What are some questions we could ask about these data? First, we might ask which of the independent variables (1-6) have effects on the dependent variables (7-11). Second, we might ask about interactions among the independent variables; e.g. does the effect of gender depend on the district? Third, we might ask about an association between the dependent variables: is a child's ranking of popularity factors (#8-11) associated with his/her personal goal (#7)?

Assume the data were collected and entered by research assistants in each of the districts, and now we have three data files. Some of our questions could be addressed separately for each file, but some could not (e.g. the effect of district). In any case, it would be poor practice to ask the same question for three separate data sets, because doing so would increase the likelihood of a type I error and at the same time reduce the power of any statistical tests we might do. For these reasons, we should put the three files together.

Consulting the guidelines in 6.4, we see that we have three data sets with the same variables and different cases, so we should append them. The first step is to look at the three sets and make sure they have the same variables in the same order.

```
> load file rural
> list variables
```

List of current variables:

Name	Type	N
gender	string(4)	149
grade	numeric8.2	149
age	numeric8.2	149
race	string(5)	149
district	string(8)	149
school	string(20)	149
goals	string(10)	149
grades	numeric8.2	149
sports	numeric8.2	149
looks	numeric8.2	149
money	numeric8.2	149

The good news is that there are no missing values – there are 149 observations on each variable. The bad news is that the rural research assistant entered gender, race, district, school, and goals as strings. For our purposes, we will need to convert them to encoded strings (see 3.5). Let's see what the suburban research assistant did.

```
> load file suburban
> list variables
```

List of current variables:

Name	Type	N
gender	numeric1.0	151
grade	numeric8.2	151
age	numeric8.2	151
race	numeric1.0	151
district	string(8)	151
school	string(20)	151
goals	string(10)	151
grades	numeric8.2	151
sports	numeric8.2	151
looks	numeric8.2	151
money	numeric8.2	151

Again there are no missing values, but gender and race have been entered as encoded strings. This means that we will have to encode those variables in the rural file before we can append the suburban file. But before we do anything, let's look at the urban file.

```
> load file urban
> list variables
```

```
List of current variables:
Name        Type            N
gender      string(4)       178
race        string(5)       178
district    string(8)       178
school      string(20)      178
goals       string(10)      178
grade       numeric8.2      178
age         numeric8.2      178
grades      numeric8.2      178
sports      numeric8.2      178
looks       numeric8.2      178
money       numeric8.2      178
```

The urban research assistant has entered the data in the same way as the rural data, but has put the variables in a different order, perhaps believing that the string variables should be together, and likewise the numeric variables. Before these three files can be appended to one another, we must:

    1. Encode gender and race in the rural and urban files.
    2. Re-order the variables in the urban file.

We need to encode district, school, and goals in all three files, so we will wait until the files are combined and do it once.

To fix the rural file, we need to know the encoding scheme that was used in the suburban file.

```
> load file suburban
> list value labels, var=gender

        var         value   label
        gender      1       boy
                    2       girl

> list value labels, var=race

        var         value   label
        race        1       other
                    2       white
```

In both cases an alphabetic encoding scheme was used. This is handy for us because it means we can let the software encode the strings in the other files. It will follow an alphabetic scheme unless we tell it to do otherwise.

```
> load file rural
> encode gender into gendernum
> encode race into racenum
```
Just to make sure, we might check the result:

```
> list value labels, var=gendernum

        var         value   label
        gendernum   1       boy
                    2       girl

> list value labels, var=racenum
```

```
var        value    label
racenum    1        other
           2        white
```

Good. Notice that the encoding operation created two new variables, gendernum and racenum. We want to substitute these for gender and race.

```
> delete gender
> rename gendernum, newname=gender
> delete race
> rename racenum, newname=race
```

The substitution has been made, but because new variables are added to the rightmost side of the spreadsheet, the new gender and race are out of order:

```
> list variables

List of current variables:
Name      Type         N
grade     numeric8.2   149
age       numeric8.2   149
district  string(8)    149
school    string(20)   149
goals     string(10)   149
grades    numeric8.2   149
sports    numeric8.2   149
looks     numeric8.2   149
money     numeric8.2   149
gender    numeric1.0   149
race      numeric1.0   149
> order variables = gender grade age race district school goals grades
  sports looks money
> save file rural
```

Now we can fix the urban file.

```
> load file urban
> encode gender into gendernum
> encode race into racenum
> delete gender
> rename gendernum, newname=gender
> delete race
> rename racenum, newname=race
> order variables = gender grade age race district school goals grades
  sports looks money
> save file urban
```

Finally we can combine the files. Urban is currently in memory, so we will append the other two.

```
> append file rural
> append file suburban
> list variables
```

```
List of current variables:
Name        Type          N
gender      numeric1.0    478
grade       numeric8.2    478
age         numeric8.2    478
race        numeric1.0    478
district    string(8)     478
school      string(20)    478
goals       string(10)    478
grades      numeric8.2    478
sports      numeric8.2    478
looks       numeric8.2    478
money       numeric8.2    478
```

Now that all the data are in one place we can finish the encoding:

```
> encode district into districtnum
> encode school into schoolnum
> encode goals into goalsnum
> delete district school goals
> rename districtnum, newname=district
> rename schoolnum, newname=school
> rename goalsnum, newname=goals
> save file popular
```

At last the data are ready to use.

Exercises

1. Using the files supplied on the web site, follow the above demonstration and combine the three files using your statistical software.

2. Which of the independent variables (1-6) seem to have effects on the dependent variables (7-11)?

3. What, if any, interactions among the independent variables are apparent? (For example, does the effect of gender depend on the district?)

4. Are there any associations among the dependent variables? (For example, is a child's ranking of popularity factors associated with his/her personal goal (#7)?)

Demonstration 7

Cutting it Close

TO MAKE A PAIR OF PANTS, you lay out a pattern on a piece of fabric, and you cut out the pattern. You sew the resulting pieces together and you have a pair of pants. What's left over is waste. It is best to lay out the pattern in such a way as to minimize waste.

Levi-Strauss makes a lot of pants. The sewing happens at the Levi-Strauss factory, but the cutting is done by five sub-contractors. Levi-Strauss sends them cloth, and they send back pants pieces. Obviously Levi-Strauss would like to get as many pieces as possible out of a given amount of cloth, and they keep track of the waste produced by each of the suppliers. Specifically, they are interested in the percentage of cloth wasted relative to what would be wasted by using computer layouts of patterns.

Suppose we have a file for each supplier with weekly waste percentages (Koopmans, 1987). We would like to be able to find out whether there are differences among the suppliers in terms of waste. Accordingly, we want to combine the five files. The question is, how do we want the data to be arranged in the combined file?

Each file has a single variable: % waste relative to the computer's performance. We could arrange the files end-to-end, like this:

```
waste%
[supplier1_week1]
[supplier1_week2]
      .
      .
      .
[supplier1_weekn]
[supplier2_week1]
      .
      .
      .
[supplier5_weekn]
```

If we did this, we would have to add a supplier number variable to each file before combining them – otherwise there would be no way to know which supplier a given measurement comes from and therefore no way to compare the suppliers. Alternatively, we could arrange the files side-by-side, like this:

```
supplier1waste%       supplier2waste%  . . .supplier5waste%
[week1]        . . .   [week1]          . . .[week1]
[week2]        . . .   [week2]          . . .[week2]
    .              .                       .
    .              .                       .
    .              .                       .
[weekn]        . . .   [weekn]          . . .[weekn]
```

Either arrangement is reasonable, and in fact we will probably want both arrangements before we're through. The path of least resistance is probably to combine the data side-by-side and then to restructure them to produce the end-to-end arrangement.

In the side-by-side arrangement we are treating each supplier's waste figures as a separate variable. These are weekly figures, so in effect each week is a case, and we are combining different variables (suppliers) on the same cases (1st week, 2nd, 3rd, etc.). From the guidelines in 7.4 we can see that a one-to-one merge is in order.

```
> load supplier1
> merge file supplier2
> merge file supplier3
> merge file supplier4
> merge file supplier5
```

Here is the result:

	supplier1	supplier2	supplier3	supplier4	supplier5	
1	1.2	16.4	12.1	11.5	24.0	
2	10.1	-6.0	9.7	10.2	-3.7	
3	-2.0	-11.6	7.4	3.8	8.2	
4	1.5	-1.3	-2.1	8.3	9.2	
5	-3.0	4.0	10.1	6.6	-9.3	
6	-0.7	17.0	4.7	10.2	8.0	
7	3.2	3.8	4.6	8.8	15.8	
8	2.7	4.3	3.9	2.7	22.3	
9	-3.2	10.4	3.6	5.1	3.1	
10	-1.7	4.2	9.6	11.2	16.8	
11	2.4	8.5	9.8	5.9	11.3	
12	0.3	6.3	6.5	13.0	12.3	
13	3.5	9.0	5.7	6.8	16.9	
14	-0.8	7.1	5.1	14.5	.	
15	19.4	4.3	3.4	5.2	.	
16	2.8	19.7	-0.8	7.3	.	
17	13.0	3.0	-3.9	7.1	.	
18	42.7	7.6	0.9	3.4	.	
19	1.4	70.2	1.5	0.7	.	
20	3.0	8.5	.	.	.	
21	2.4	6.0	.	.	.	
22	1.3	2.9	.	.	.	

(Negative values indicate that the cutters wasted less cloth than the computer would have done.) Notice that the one-to-one merge works even when files don't have the same number of cases. When this happens, merge fills out the data set with missing values.

Now let's take a look at the data. Which supplier produces the least waste? How much week-to-week variation is there? One approach to such questions is an error bar graph:

```
> plot errorbars, vars are supplier1 supplier2 supplier3 supplier4 supplier5
```

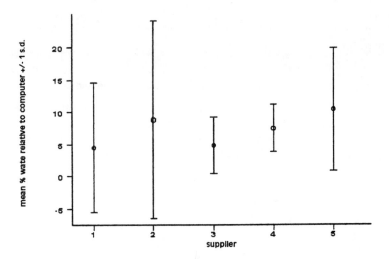

Another perspective comes from a box plot:

```
> plot box, vars are supplier1 supplier2 supplier3 supplier4 supplier5
```

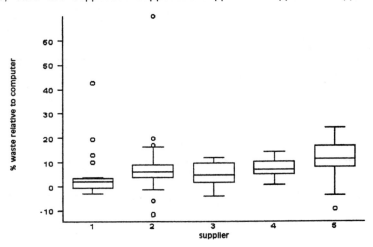

These graphs suggest that some suppliers are more efficient than others. Are the differences among them statistically significant? To answer this we could perform a one-way analysis of variance, and perhaps a Scheffé test. For that most software wants the data arranged scorewise, and they are currently casewise, so we will

```
> save file waste_cwise
```

because we may want the casewise version of the data again. Now we need to create a case identifier variable:

```
> create week, values = $n          [ $n is the row number system variable ]
```

Here's what we have:

```
week            [case identifier]
supplier1       [dep. var. (waste) for 1st level of ind. var. (supplier)]
supplier2       [dep. var. (waste) for 2nd level of ind. var. (supplier)]
supplier3       [dep. var. (waste) for 3rd level of ind. var. (supplier)]
supplier4       [dep. var. (waste) for 4th level of ind. var. (supplier)]
supplier5       [dep. var. (waste) for 5th level of ind. var. (supplier)]
```

We want to wind up with:

```
week            [case identifier]
supplier        [independent variable]
waste           [dependent variable]
```

```
> restructure scorewise / id=week
    / grouping var=supplier, values=1,2,3,4,5
    / dep var=waste, prefix=supplier
```

Now the data look like this:

	week	suppli	waste
1	1	1	1.2
2	1	2	16.4
3	1	3	12.1
4	1	4	11.5
5	1	5	24.0
6	2	1	10.1
7	2	2	-6.0
8	2	3	9.7
9	2	4	10.2
10	2	5	-3.7
11	3	1	-2.0
12	etc.		

```
> anova factor = supplier depvar = waste
```

	Sum of Squares	df	Mean Square	F	Sig.
Between Groups	450.921	4	112.730	1.160	.334
Within Groups	8749.088	90	97.212		
Total	9200.009	94			

The non-significant F statistic tells us that the differences among the five pants-pieces suppliers are not reliable. If we were to collect waste data for another stretch of time it is not unlikely that the relative efficiencies of the five suppliers would be different. Therefore, before Levi-Strauss lowers the boom on supplier 5 they should collect more data.

Displaying Data in Tables

Chapter Outline

The most common way of displaying data is in a table. There are two basic kinds:
1. Frequency tables show the numbers of cases belonging to each of two or more categories or combinations of categories.
2. Summary tables show the mean of a quantitative variable corresponding to each of two or more categories or combinations of categories.

STATISTICAL SOFTWARE computes statistics, of course, but it also prepares and displays summaries of our data. If I could have only one of these functions, I would choose the second. Being able to make tables and graphs will let us get a pretty good idea of what's going on in our data, even if we can't test the reliability of these effects. Looking at our data is an essential part of analysis, and tables and graphs also give us a way to communicate our results to others. In this chapter and the next we will take a more detailed look at tables and graphs.

8.1 Frequency tables

Suppose we ask 200 people two questions:

    1. Do you drink coffee?
    2. Do you smoke?

Our data will look like this:

	smoke?	coffee?
1	yes	yes
2	yes	yes
3	yes	no
4	no	yes
5	yes	no
6	yes	yes
7	yes	yes
8	no	no
9	no	yes
10	yes	yes
etc.		

125

Respondents 1 and 2 smoke and drink coffee, respondent 3 smokes but doesn't drink coffee, respondent 4 doesn't smoke but does drink coffee, and so on. Looking at the raw data isn't very enlightening, so we do some *tabulating*[11], or counting, and put our results in a *table*:

smoke?	count	%
yes	75	37.5
no	125	62.5
total	200	100.0

Specifically, this is a one-way frequency (count) table. It shows how many times each value of some categorical variable (smoke?) occurs in the sample. What about the other variable? We can make a table for it, too:

coffee?	count	%
yes	131	65.5
no	69	34.5
total	200	100.0

(Bear in mind that both tables contain the same 200 people.) Each of these tables shows the distribution of a single categorical variable. The genius of tables emerges when we want to look at the *joint distribution* of two categorical variables.

Here is a *two-way frequency table*, also known as a *contingency table*, *cross-tabulation*, or *bivariate frequency distribution*:

	smokes	doesn't smoke	total
drinks coffee	47	84	131
doesn't drink coffee	28	41	69
total	75	125	200

The numbers are all *frequencies*, or counts. The first *cell* shows that there are 47 people in this sample who both drink coffee and smoke. That's nice, but usually we want to know: 47 out of how many? For this we look to one of the totals. For example, the total for the "drinks coffee" row shows that there are 131 coffee drinkers; so 47 out of 131 coffee drinkers also smoke. Likewise, the total for the "smokes" column shows that there are 75 smokers; so 47 out of 75 smokers are also coffee drinkers. Finally, the grand total is 200; so 47 out of 200 people sampled both drink coffee and smoke. Notice that the row and column totals in this table are the frequencies from the one-way tables we saw earlier.

Thinking about things in this "how many out of how many" way is easier if we use proportions or percentages. Here is the same table with the cell frequencies expressed as percentages of the row totals:

---

[11] *Tabula* is Latin for *tablet*. A Roman's tablet was a smooth wax surface; our tablet is a pad of paper. Either way, a tablet is a handy thing for counting, for example by making tally marks.

%	smokes	doesn't smoke	total
drinks coffee	35.9	64.1	100.0
doesn't drink coffee	40.6	59.4	100.0
total	37.5	62.5	100.0

> Frequencies are often more useful when they are expressed as percentages.
>
> Here, they are percentages of the row totals.

Now the 47 out of 131 becomes 35.9%; that is, 35.9% of coffee drinkers (in the sample) are smokers. Likewise, 40.6% of non-coffee drinkers are smokers, and 37.5% of the sample are smokers. When we compute the percentages by row, we learn about the column variable (smoking): most people in our sample, whether they drink coffee or not, don't smoke. What if we want to know the percentage of smokers who are coffee drinkers? For that we need to compute the percentages by column rather than by row. Here is the same table with the cell frequencies expressed as percentages of the column totals:

%	smokes	doesn't smoke	total
drinks coffee	62.7	67.2	65.5
doesn't drink coffee	37.3	32.8	34.5
total	100.0	100.0	100.0

> Here the frequencies are expressed as percentages of the column totals.

Now the 47 out of 75 becomes 62.7%; that is, 62.7% of smokers (in the sample) are coffee drinkers. Likewise, 67.2% of non-smokers are coffee drinkers, and 65.5% of the sample are coffee drinkers. When we compute the percentages by column, we learn about the row variable (coffee drinking): most people in our sample, whether they smoke or not, drink coffee. Finally, what if we want to know the percentage of the sample who are both smokers and coffee drinkers? For that we need to compute the percentages cell by cell. Here is the same table with the cell frequencies expressed as percentages of the grand total:

%	smokes	doesn't smoke	total
drinks coffee	23.5	42.0	65.5
doesn't drink coffee	14.0	20.5	34.5
total	37.5	62.5	100.0

> Here the frequencies are expressed as percentages of the table total.

Now the 47 out of 200 becomes 23.5%; that is, 23.5% of the sample are both smokers and coffee drinkers. When we compute the percentages by cell, we learn about the combinations of the row and column variables.

To complicate things a bit further, suppose we had asked a third question:

3. Do you eat meat?

Then our data would look like this:

smoke?	coffee?	meat?
yes	yes	yes
yes	yes	yes
yes	no	no
no	yes	yes
yes	no	yes
yes	yes	yes
yes	yes	yes
no	no	no
no	yes	no
yes	yes	yes

We can still make one- and two-way tables, but to see the joint distribution of all three variables, we need a three-way table, which might look like this:

> A three-way table shows the frequencies (or percentages) in each combination of the values of three categorical variables.

		eats meat?							
		yes				no			
		smokes?				smokes?			
		yes	no	total		yes	no	total	total
drinks coffee?	yes	42	59	101		5	25	30	131
	no	25	23	48		3	18	21	69
	total	67	82	149		8	43	51	200

A three-way table is in fact two two-way tables, one for each value of the higher-order variable, which in this case is meat? We could make two other 3-way tables with these data: one with smokes? and one with coffee? as the higher-order variable. Which table(s) we make depends on what question(s) we have.

One-way, two-way, three-way... four-way? In principle, there is no limit to the number of variables you can cross-tabulate. In practice, it is hard enough to make sense of a three-way table, and when a table gets big it risks becoming number salad.

8.2   Summary tables

Cross-tabulations are strictly for categorical variables, but they are not the only kind of table. Suppose that in addition to asking whether respondents drink coffee, smoke, and eat meat, we also ask their age. Now we might ask whether coffee-drinkers tend to be older or younger than non-drinkers:

age	mean	s.d.	n
coffee-drinkers	47.3	16.2	131
non-drinkers	34.8	15.3	69
total	43.0	15.9	200

> *A one-way summary table summarizes a quantitative variable for each value of a categorical variable.*

This is a *summary table*, so called because it contains summary measures – in this case means and standard deviations. Furthermore, this is a *one-way* summary table, because it provides summary measures of a quantitative variable (age) corresponding to each of the values of one categorical variable. This table tells us that the 131 coffee drinkers in the sample have a mean age of 47.3, with a standard deviation of 16.2, and that the 69 non-drinkers have a mean age of 34.8 with a standard deviation of 15.3, and that the sample as a whole has a mean age of 43.0 with a standard deviation of 15.9. Notice that the frequencies (n) are numbers we have seen before. The summary table incorporates a table of frequencies, but that is not its primary purpose. In a frequency table, we are asking *How many cases are there for each value of the (categorical) variable?* while in a summary table we are asking *What is the ___ (mean, median, s.d., etc.) of the quantitative variable for each group defined by the categorical variable?*

A two-way summary table follows the same logic:

mean s.d. frequency	smokers	non-smokers	total
coffee drinkers	39.6 14.8 47	51.6 16.9 84	47.3 16.2 131
non-drinkers	34.3 15.2 28	35.1 15.4 41	34.8 15.3 69
total	37.6 15.0 75	46.2 16.4 125	43.0 15.9 200

Now instead of having separate columns for mean, s.d., and n, we have all three in the same cell. If we wanted only the mean we could have that.

I can't stress too strongly how important it is to be clear about the difference between frequency tables and summary tables. You'll probably make a mistake once in a while; here's what your output will look like if you cross-tabulate a categorical and a quantitative variable:

	female	male	total
23	1	1	2
24	1	0	1
26	0	1	1
29	1	2	3
30	0	1	1
32	1	0	1
35	0	1	1
36	2	1	3
etc.			

(age)

The cell frequencies are small, and many are zero, because there aren't many cases for each age. Likewise, there are many rows because there are many values of age; this is characteristic of quantitative variables. Don't attempt to interpret a table like this; it's worthless. Instead, do the right thing: make a one-way summary table of age by sex.

age	mean	s.d.	n
female	48.3	1.7	85
male	45.9	11.2	65
total	47.3	12.1	150

8.3   Exercises

1. Suppose we administer the following survey to 50 randomly selected people:

1. Do you have a pet?   (yes/no)
2. What is your marital status? (single/married/divorced/widowed)
3. Do you have a car?   (yes/no)
4. How old are you?   (# of years)

Here are some (imaginary) data:

pet	mstat	car	age	pet	mstat	car	age
y	s	y	35	n	s	y	21
n	w	y	21	n	m	y	30
y	s	n	54	y	s	n	13
y	s	n	62	n	d	y	25
n	m	y	85	n	s	y	44
n	m	y	36	n	s	y	38
n	m	y	73	y	s	n	72
y	d	y	47	y	m	y	52
y	m	n	84	y	m	y	41
n	d	y	59	n	s	n	11
n	m	y	20	n	m	n	41
n	s	n	43	y	s	y	60
y	s	y	26	y	m	n	70
n	s	y	34	n	d	n	55
n	m	y	47	n	m	n	26
n	d	y	38	n	s	y	33
y	m	n	24	y	m	y	27
y	s	n	15	y	d	y	38
y	w	y	77	y	s	y	20

pet	mstat	car	age		pet	mstat	car	age
y	w	y	69		n	m	n	63
n	s	y	23		y	w	n	84
y	m	y	32		y	w	n	79
n	m	y	50		n	s	y	46
y	d	n	31		y	w	n	80
y	d	y	32		n	s	y	31

Answer the following questions using pencil and paper.

1. Make a one-way frequency table for each of the categorical variables (pet, mstat, car). (Why shouldn't you make a frequency table for age?)

2. Make a one-way summary table of age by pet.

3. Make a one-way summary table of age by mstat.

4. Cross-tabulate pet and car, using frequencies. Make pet the row (side) variable and car the column (top) variable.

5. Make another table identical to the last one but expressing each frequency as a percentage of its row total.

6. a) What percentage of pet owners have a car? b)What percentage of those who do not have a pet have a car?

7. Make another table identical to the last one but expressing each frequency as a percentage of its column total.

8. a) What percentage of car owners have a pet? b) Why is this not the same as #6a?

9. Make another table identical to the last one but expressing each frequency as a percentage of the table total.

10. a) What percentage of the sample have both a pet and a car? b) Why is this not the same as #6a or #8a?

11. Cross tabulate pet and mstat, using frequencies. Make mstat the row (side) variable and pet the column (top) variable.

12. Make the appropriate table of percentages to answer each of the following: a) What percentage of pet owners are married? b) What percentage of the sample are single people without pets? c) What percentage of divorced people have pets?

13. Make a summary table (means only) of age by pet and car. Make pet the row (side) variable and car the column (top) variable.

14. a) What is the mean age of non-car owners? b) What is the mean age of pet owners? c) What is the mean age of people who have a pet and a car? d) What is the mean age of the sample? e) Which of these means can you find in #2? f) Will these means change if you make car the row variable and pet the column variable?

15. Make a 3-way cross-tabulation of pet, car and mstat. Make pet the column variable, mstat the row variable, and car the higher-order variable (see example in 8.1).

16. a) How many widowed pet owners do not have cars? b) What percentage of widowed pet owners do not have cars?

17. Make a 3-way summary table of age (means only) by pet, car, and mstat.

18. What is the mean age of widowed pet owners who do not have cars?

19. Repeat the above exercises using a computer.

Displaying Data in Graphs

Chapter Outline

There are many kinds of graphs available for displaying data, and it is important to use the right one:
1. Histograms show the distribution of a quantitative variable.
2. Bar graphs show the mean of a quantitative variable for each level of a categorical variable.
3. Box plots show the distribution of a quantitative variable for each level of a categorical variable.
4. Line graphs show the value or mean of a quantitative variable for each value of a time-related independent variable.
5. Scatter plots display the values of two quantitative variables for each case individually.

THERE ARE MANY GRAPHS in this book, and you have undoubtedly noticed that they are powerful analytic tools as well as an effective way to communicate about data. Like many useful things, they have great potential for misuse and abuse. In this chapter we will look more closely at the most common kinds of graphs, paying particular attention to the question of when and how to use each one.

9.1   Histograms

How do we graph the distribution of a variable? Here are the school day length data from Ch. 1 (daylength.dat) again:

The bars in a histogram have no spaces between them.

There is only one variable in a histogram.

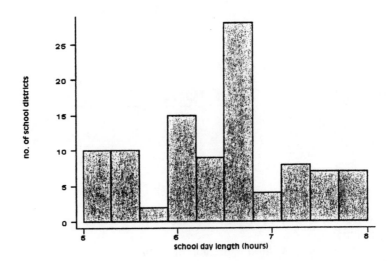

The bars of a histogram are called *bins* because their height reflects the number of cases in them. As a rule of thumb, the number of bins should be roughly the square root of the number of cases. The x-axis shows the value, or range of values, of the variable that go in each bin. The y-axis can be the *number* (count, frequency) of cases in a bin or the *proportion* of the total number of cases that fall in each bin. Whichever kind of y-axis we use, the pattern of ups and downs in a histogram tells us the *shape* – symmetric, skewed, level, etc. – of the variable's distribution.

9.2   Bar graphs

Cuckoos lay their eggs in other species' nests. When the eggs hatch the 'host' parents raise the young cuckoos. The trick, from the cuckoos' point of view, is to get the host parents to adopt the cuckoos' eggs. Cuckoos return to and mate in the same territory every year, and lay their eggs in the nests of a particular host species. From an evolutionary perspective, this specialization in a particular geographic region and host species means that natural selection will favor those cuckoos who lay eggs most likely to be adopted by the host species. Latter (1902) measured the lengths of cuckoo eggs in the nests of six host species. His data look like this:

meadow pipit	tree pipit	hedge sparrow	robin	pied wagtail	wren
19.65	21.05	20.85	21.05	21.05	19.85
20.05	21.85	21.65	21.85	21.85	20.05
20.65	22.05	22.05	22.05	21.85	20.25
etc.					

We want to know whether the mean length of cuckoo eggs differs from one host species to another. We could ask for a one-way summary table (try it; use cuckoo.dat), or we could ask for a bar graph:

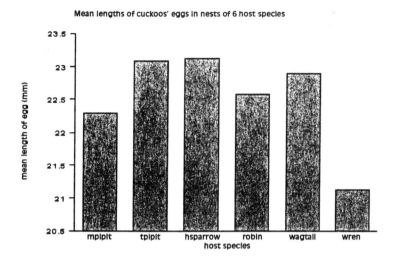

Mean lengths of cuckoos' eggs in nests of 6 host species

A bar graph shows the value of some quantitative summary measure (mean, median, sum, etc.) on the y-axis, with a separate bar for each value of a categorical variable. In this case, each bar's height represents the mean length of cuckoo eggs laid in the nests of a given host species. For example, cuckoo eggs in pied wagtail nests have a mean length of 22.9 mm, while those laid in wren nests are only 21.1 mm long. To put it differently, the eggs cuckoos lay in wagtail nests are about 8.5% longer than the eggs they lay in wren nests. But look at those bars: the wagtail bar is at least three times as high as the wren bar. Representing a difference of 8.5% as one of over 300% may be acceptable in advertising, but not in science. What do we do?

The graph above is what I got when I asked the software for a bar graph of the cuckoo data. The key to the gross exaggeration of small differences is the y-axis. Notice that it begins, not at zero, but at 20.5. If we force the software to begin at zero, the deception disappears:

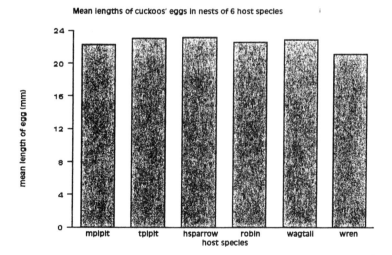

Mean lengths of cuckoos' eggs in nests of 6 host species

The first graph makes us say "Wow!," but this one may not get even a "hmmm..."

Nevertheless, this is the correct way to graph these data[1], because the relative heights of the bars reflect the relative lengths of the eggs.

9.3   The box-and-whisker plot

The bar graphs above gave us only means. If we'd like to know something about the distribution of the variable as well, we can use a box-and-whisker plot (box plot, for short).

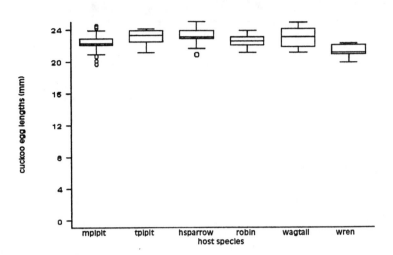

Each box shows the distribution of the y-variable for a given value of the x-variable.

The box plot is very useful, but it needs a little explanation. The line through the middle (roughly) of each box is the median score; the bottom of the box is the 25th percentile and the top of the box is the 75th percentile. (The distance between these percentiles is the interquartile range, a measure of variability). The horizontal lines at the ends of the whiskers sticking out of the box mark the upper and lower adjacent values. The upper adjacent value is the highest score that is less than or equal to the 75th percentile plus 1.5 times the interquartile range, and the lower adjacent value is the lowest score that is greater than or equal to the 25th percentile minus 1.5 times the interquartile range (for a more detailed discussion see Tukey, 1977). The purpose of the adjacent values is to give us a sense of where most of the scores are and whether there are any extreme values. Any score beyond the adjacent values would be plotted by itself. For most of the boxes above, the adjacent values are also the highest and lowest scores, indicating no extreme scores, but the meadow pipit and hedge sparrow have a few. The overall configuration of a box and its whiskers tell us at a glance the shape of the distribution of values that it represents. The distribution of egg lengths from robin nests, for example, is fairly symmetric: the median is close to the center of the box (i.e. the same distance from the 25th and the 75th percentiles) and its whiskers are approximately the same length. The tree pipit box, on the other hand, shows a positively skewed distribution (the median is much closer to the 75th than to the 25th percentile, and the upper whisker is much shorter than the lower).

Box plots are like bar graphs in that the y-axis represents a quantitative variable (and should therefore begin at zero) and each box corresponds to the value of a categorical vari-

---

[1] If you look in today's newspaper you will probably find a graph without a zero, but this does not justify the practice. Some people argue that leaving out the zero makes better use of the space in a graph and makes differences between means clearer. Indeed, it does, but only by making differences look bigger than they are. Unless you think you can specifically justify such distortion, use a zero.

able. But while the bar graph displays only a single summary measure, the box plot gives us a measure of central tendency (the median) and of variability (the interquartile range), shows the skewness of the distribution, and alerts us to outliers. A bar graph may be a better choice for presenting results to an unsophisticated audience, but as a tool for exploring data a box plot is much more useful.

9.4   The line graph

Here are some Olympic high jump data:

```
year    highest jump (inches)
1896    71.25
1900    74.8
1904    71
1908    75
1912    76
etc.
```

Have Olympians been jumping higher over the years? We could inspect the data, or we could make a *line graph*, which is especially useful for showing how a quantitative variable changes over time:

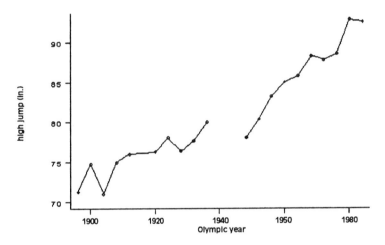

> The line makes it easier to see the order (in terms of the x-variable) of the data points.

This graph shows the highest jump in each Olympic year. The little circles are called *plotting symbols*, and each one represents a single *data point*, in this case a jump. The plotting symbols are connected by a line to show their order and to make whatever trend might be present more visible. In these data there is a clear upward trend: on the whole, jumps get higher as time goes on. The gap in the middle of the line reflects the fact that there were no Olympics during the second world war.

Notice that the y-axis does not begin at zero. This is usually the case in line graphs, and it is usually acceptable, even preferable, because the main purpose of a line graph is to show trends rather than differences. But while we don't worry about the y-axis of a line graph, we do need to be careful with the x-axis. Here's another line graph:

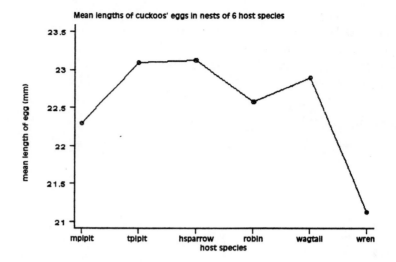

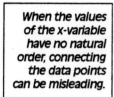

When the values of the x-variable have no natural order, connecting the data points can be misleading.

These are the cuckoo data again, in a line graph version of the bar graph we saw earlier. The difference is that the line connecting the data points implies an order or sequence in time that doesn't exist. The meadow pipit doesn't come before the tree pipit in the way that 1968 comes before 1972. Perhaps we can impose some order by arranging the birds this way:

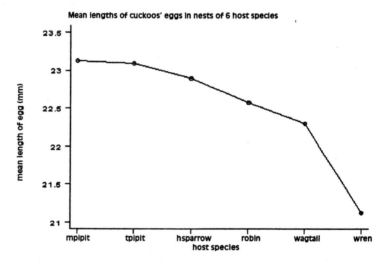

Now we can say that cuckoo egg length goes down over six host species. But we could just as easily arrange the data so that egg length goes up over six host species. Either way it's no good. Putting the data points in order doesn't create what a line graph implies: an ordered x-variable.

Another important use of line graphs is to look at two or more trends simultaneously. For example, here are some data from a test of the effectiveness of the resin of a certain tropical tree as a termite poison (Meinwald & Messer, 1990). The experimenters put 25 termites in a dish with a piece of filter paper containing some resin. There were eight dishes with 5 mg. of resin and another eight dishes with 10 mg. The termites still alive in each dish were counted on 13 out of 15 consecutive days.

dish	dose	day 1	2	3	4	5	6	7	8	9	10	11	12	13	14	15
1	5	25	24	.	22	18	17	15	14	.	13	13	12	11	11	11
2	5	25	25	.	25	21	20	17	15	.	15	15	12	11	11	11
3	5	25	25	.	24	23	21	20	19	.	16	13	13	13	13	12
4	5	25	25	.	25	24	22	22	21	.	20	18	13	13	13	12
5	5	25	25	.	22	19	18	17	14	.	13	11	11	8	8	5
6	5	25	25	.	23	20	17	16	15	.	15	13	11	11	10	9
7	5	25	25	.	24	23	22	20	19	.	16	15	11	9	7	6
8	5	25	25	.	23	19	17	16	14	.	12	12	11	11	11	10
1	10	25	24	.	23	22	21	19	18	.	18	18	18	17	17	16
2	10	25	25	.	23	20	19	18	18	.	17	17	16	15	14	13
3	10	25	24	.	12	6	5	4	2	.	2	1	1	1	1	1
4	10	25	24	.	14	10	7	4	3	.	3	2	2	2	1	0
5	10	25	24	.	16	9	6	5	1	.	0	0	0	0	0	0
6	10	25	24	.	7	3	1	1	1	.	0	0	0	0	0	0
7	10	25	18	.	4	3	1	1	0	.	0	0	0	0	0	0
8	10	25	21	.	17	9	7	7	7	.	5	4	3	3	3	3

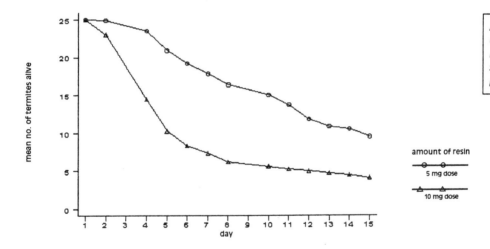

A line graph can contain two (or more) separate series of data points.

amount of resin

5 mg dose

10 mg dose

This line graph plots the two doses separately. The stuff to the right of the graph is called a *legend*; it tells us which line represents which group. The larger dose of resin doesn't necessarily kill more termites (we don't know for sure where the upper line is going, but it is possible that after another week, say, both doses would have killed all the termites), but clearly the larger dose kills termites faster.

There were no observations on days 3 and 9, but there are no gaps in the lines. Why not? In the high jump graph there had to be a gap for 1940 and 1944, because we have no idea how high the jumps would have been had the Olympics been held in those years. In the case of the termites, however, we do have a pretty good idea how many termites would have been alive on days 3 and 9. Assuming termites don't rise from the dead and don't reproduce while they are busy being poisoned, the number of termites alive on a given day cannot be greater than the number alive on the previous day or less than the number alive on the next day.

9.5   The scatter plot

If we have data in which cases are measured on two quantitative variables, we generally use a scatter plot. For example, here are average weekly household expenditures (in pounds) on alcohol and tobacco in the 11 regions of the U.K. (Central Statistical Office, 1981):

region	alcohol	tobacco
North	£6.47	£4.03
Yorkshire	6.13	3.76
Northeast	6.19	3.77
East Midlands	4.89	3.34
West Midlands	5.63	3.47
East Anglia	4.52	2.92
Southeast	5.89	3.20
Southwest	4.79	2.71
Wales	5.27	3.53
Scotland	6.08	4.51
Northern Ireland	4.02	4.56

Each case is a region, and it has been measured on two quantitative variables. Unlike other graphs, in a scatter plot it is not always obvious which variable should be assigned to which axis, so let's try it both ways:

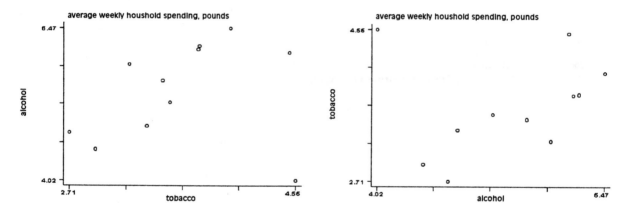

Each data point in a scatter plot is a case, so in these graphs each dot represents a region, and its position represents that region's values on the two quantitative variables, i.e. alcohol and tobacco expenditures. The scatter plot shows the relation between those variables. These graphs show that alcohol and tobacco expenditures are positively correlated: regions that spend more on alcohol tend to spend more on tobacco. Notice that we can see this in both graphs; in fact, the two are simply mirror images of one another.

How strong is the relation between alcohol and tobacco expenditures? We could compute a correlation coefficient, or we could plot a regression line.

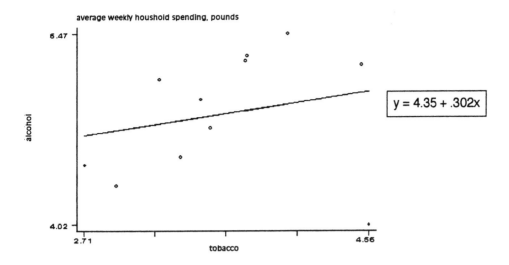

The regression equation at the right of the graph is the equation of the line: it has an intercept of 4.35 and a slope of .302. We can use this equation (or the line) to predict alcohol expenditure. For example, a region that spends £4.00 a week on tobacco should spend 4.35 + .302(4.00), or £5.56 a week on alcohol. The (x,y) pair (4.00, 5.56) is a point that the regression line passes through, and it will also pass through any other point predicted by the equation. We can think of the line, then, as the set of predicted values of y (alcohol expenditures) for all possible values of x (tobacco expenditures).

How good are these predictions? We can see that the line comes within a few pence of a few of the points, but it misses most of them by rather more than that. Indeed, it misses the point at the lower right by roughly two pounds. This visual inspection is confirmed by the regression analysis, which produces a statistic, R^2, that measures the proportion of the variance in y that is accounted for by x; in this case $R^2 = .05$. Not very impressive. But before we conclude that there is very little relation between alcohol and tobacco spending, let's look again at the scatter plot. What's the story with that point down in the lower right corner? Is this is a region where people smoke like fiends and drink very little? Or is it a region where tobacco is expensive and alcohol is cheap? We don't know, but either way we can see that this region is exerting a strong influence on the regression line. Doesn't it look like the line ought to be steeper? Perhaps it would be if we removed that one anomalous region from the analysis.

To do this we need to know which region it is. One way to find out is to change the plotting symbol from a dot to the name of the region:

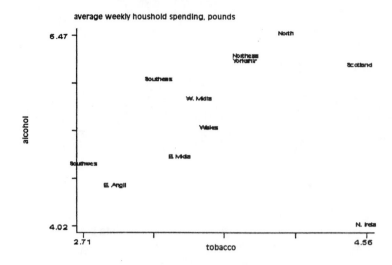

The outlying region, numerically and geographically, is Northern Ireland. Now we can repeat the regression analysis excluding Northern Ireland (see 4.6).

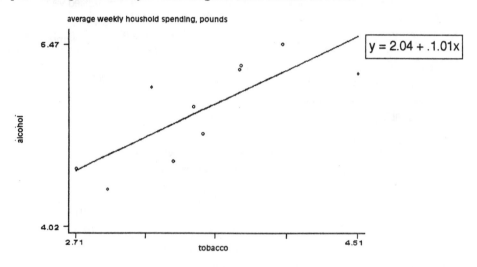

Our expectation was correct. Without Northern Ireland pulling it down the regression line has swung up, and as a result it comes much closer to most of the points. This is reflected in the value of R^2, which is now .62. This means that tobacco spending is a pretty good predictor of alcohol spending if Northern Ireland is excluded.

9.6   Exercises

1. Re-graph the histogram in 9.1 with the same number of bins (10) but with proportion (rather than frequency) on the y-axis..

2. Re-graph the histogram with different numbers of bins, such as 4, 7, 9, 12, 20, 30. What happens?

3. Experiment with the number of ticks on the x-axis.

4. In the tobacco/alcohol spending example, would we reach the same conclusions if we regressed tobacco (y) on alcohol (x)?

5. Why can we not conclude that "Tobacco spending is a pretty good predictor of alcohol spending except in Northern Ireland?"

Collapsing Data Sets

Chapter Outline

Often the analysis we want to perform requires not our raw data but counts, totals, means, proportions, or the like. In such cases we must *collapse* the data set.

1. If we have two or more measures on a single variable for each case, we can collapse the data to get a single summary measure per case.

2. We can compute more than one summary measure of a collapsed variable.

3. If for each case we have two or more measures on a single variable at each level of an independent variable, we can collapse the data to get one or more summary measure(s) per case at each level of the independent variable.

4. If for each case we have two or more measures on two dependent variables, we can collapse the data to get one or more summary measure(s) per case for each dependent variable.

O FTEN THE DATA we have are not the data we want for a particular purpose. Suppose we want to quantify the course of the common cold. We recruit three healthy, cold-free volunteers, simultaneously infect all of them with the same rhinovirus, and measure their symptoms every day until all are recovered. We measure symptoms by means of a made-up (but perfectly reasonable) variable: the Cold Symptom Severity Index, or CSSI. The CSSI is obtained from the

Cold Symptom Inventory	0	1	2	3
1. Fever	none	low	med.	high
2. Runny nose	none	mild	mod.	severe
3. Sneezing	none	mild	mod.	severe
4. Watery eyes	none	mild	mod.	severe
5. Sore throat	none	mild	mod.	severe
6. Cough	none	mild	mod.	severe
7. Headache	none	mild	mod.	severe
8. Aches & pains	none	mild	mod.	severe

The volunteer circles the severity of each symptom, and we score the responses according to the numbers at the head of each column and then add the scores. For example:

Cold Symptom Inventory	0	1	2	3
1. Fever	(none)	low	med.	high
2. Runny nose	none	(mild)	mod.	severe
3. Sneezing	none	(mild)	mod.	severe
4. Watery eyes	none	mild	(mod.)	severe
5. Sore throat	none	mild	mod.	(severe)
6. Cough	none	mild	(mod.)	severe
7. Headache	none	mild	(mod.)	severe
8. Aches & pains	(none)	mild	mod.	severe
column totals:	0	2	6	3
CSSI = 11				

Someone with no symptoms will have a score of zero, while someone who thinks it can't get any worse will have a score of 24 (3 points for each of 8 symptoms). In this way the CSSI measures both the number and the severity of the symptoms. Every day we take each volunteer's CSSI, and our data set will look like this:

```
day    volunteer    CSSI
1      1            0
1      2            0
1      3            0
2      1            2
2      2            2
2      3            0
.
.
.
5      1            9
5      2            15
5      3            12
etc.
```

Ultimately we want to know how the CSSI went up and down over the course of the study. A reasonable thing to do would be to graph our data:

```
>plot line, y=cssi, x=day, by volunteer
```

a multiple line graph

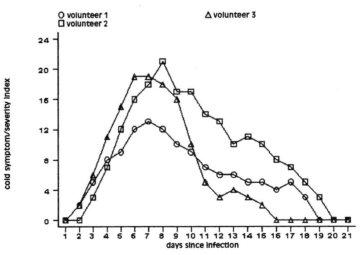

The question is, whose CSSI should we look at? What we have here is three individual CSSIs for each day, but to summarize these data we might want a single mean CSSI for each day. (This would be particularly true if we had many volunteers – imagine what the graph would look like with 20 or 30 lines in it!) To get this we have to *collapse*, or *aggregate*, the data set. The idea of collapsing is simple and always the same, but the uses of this tool can get fairly complex. We will start with the simplest case.

10.1 The simplest case

Collapsing a data set replaces the current data with the collapsed data, so our first step is always the same:

```
> save file cold
```

Do this even if you can't imagine ever needing the original data again, because (a) you never know and (b) if you collapse the wrong way, you'll want to be able to go back to the beginning and do it again.

Now we're ready:

```
> collapse mean_cssi=mean(cssi), by day
day     mean_cssi
1       0
2       1.33
.
.
5       12.0
.
.
```

Collapsing a data set makes it smaller and replaces the variables of the collapsed variable with summary values (e.g. means).

Our command said: compute the mean of cssi for each different value of day. In the process, three things happened. First, the variable cssi was replaced by mean_cssi; the software automatically attached the prefix mean_ to the variable we asked it to collapse. Second, the variable volunteer disappeared. We no longer know anything about individuals, only about the sample as a whole. Third, we have fewer observations – one third as many, to be exact.

Collapsing the data in this way allows us to see more clearly what we've got:

```
> plot line, y=mean_cssi, x=day
```

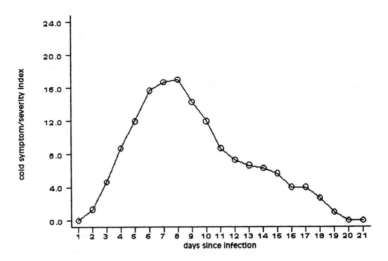

This graph shows the general trend of a cold: a day or two of latency, rapid development and worsening of symptoms, rapid initial recovery, more gradual final recovery.

Before we start making things more complicated, let's look at what we've just done in a formal way. We started out with three variables: an independent variable (day), a dependent variable (cssi) and a case identifier (volunteer). We collapsed these three variables into two: an independent variable (day), and a summary measure (mean_cssi) computed from the dependent variable.

10.2   Adding a second summary measure

Collapsing the data allowed us to make a graph that nicely summarizes the course of the cold. But look again at the graph of the original data. The three volunteers' colds are similar – which is captured by the second graph – but they are not the same, and there is no hint of this in the second graph. A useful compromise is to graph not just the mean CSSI for each day but the variability of the CSSI as well. This is usually done by adding *error bars* to the plotting symbols representing the means. An error bar is a line that extends a distance of (usually) one standard error or standard deviation above and below a mean, showing graphically the variability of the scores summarized by that mean. To make error bars we need standard deviations, which we can get by collapsing the original data:

```
> load file cold                    [good thing we didn't throw it away]
> collapse mean_cssi=mean(cssi) sdev_cssi=sd(cssi), by day

day   mean_cssi      sdev_cssi

1     0              0
2     1.33           1.15
.
.
5     12.0           3.00
.
.
```

```
> graph y=mean_cssi x=day error=sdev_cssi, line errorbar
```

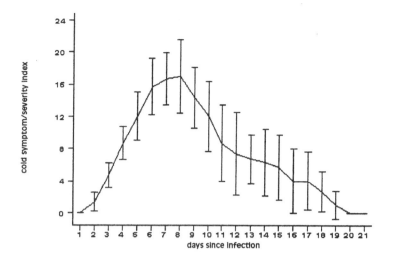

The line plots the means and the error bars show the standard deviations.

The means are represented by the points where the error bars intersect the connecting line. (When there are error bars plotting symbols are unnecessary.) This graph shows that the cssi varies more in the middle and later stages than in the early stage of a cold, and gives us a rough idea of how much variation there is among the volunteers.

10.3   Adding a second independent variable

Now that we know something about the course of the cold, we might ask what happens if we don't let the cold run its course. Is there anything that can prevent, shorten, or moderate the cold? There's certainly no shortage of candidates, from chicken soup to zinc to echinacea, but to keep things simple let's test an imaginary substance called ZP32. Our procedure is the same, but we add a second group of volunteers. Both groups begin taking pills, which they are told may be ZP32 and may be a placebo, when their first symptoms appear and continue taking them until all symptoms are gone. Our data look like this:

day	volunteer	group	cssi
1	1	placebo	0
1	2	placebo	0
1	3	placebo	0
1	4	drug	0
1	5	drug	0
1	6	drug	0
2	1	placebo	2
2	2	placebo	2
2	3	placebo	0
2	4	drug	3
2	5	drug	0
2	6	drug	1
etc.			

Again we will summarize the data by computing means, but this time we want the mean CSSI for each day for each group. Collapsing the data will do the trick:

> A data set can be collapsed in two ways (i.e. by two independent variables) at once.

```
> collapse mean_cssi=mean(cssi), by day group
day     group           mean_cssi
1       placebo             0.0
1       drug                0.0
2       placebo             1.3
2       drug                1.3
3       placebo             4.7
3       drug                4.0
etc.

> plot line, y=mean_cssi, x=day, by group
```

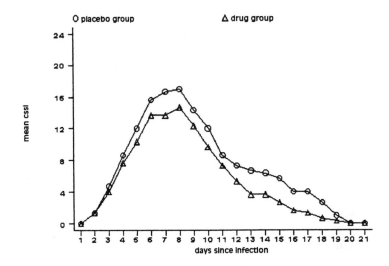

Evidently ZP32 is not the long-awaited cure for the common cold, but it does seem to reduce the severity and duration of colds.

10.4 Adding a second dependent variable

We might object to the way the Cold Symptoms Inventory is scored on the grounds that in creating a single score (the CSSI) we ignore the distinction between how many symptoms the patient has and how severe those symptoms are. A CSSI of 6, for example, could represent either two severe symptoms or six mild symptoms. If we think the distinction is important, we could score the CSI differently. First we count the symptoms that the patient reports. If s/he reports a severe headache, mild cough, and medium fever, s/he has three symptoms. Second, we compute the median rating (i.e. mild, moderate, severe). Now instead of a single index that combines number and severity of symptoms, we have a symptom count that is not influenced by severity, and a measure of severity that is not influenced by the number of symptoms.

day	vol_id	cssi	#symptoms	med_severity
1	1	0	0	0
1	2	0	0	0
1	3	0	0	0
2	1	2	1	2
2	2	2	2	1
2	3	0	0	0
3	1	5	2	2.5
3	2	6	3	2
3	3	3	3	1
4	1	8	4	2
4	2	11	4	2.67
4	3	7	3	2.33
5	1	9	3	3
5	2	15	5	3
5	3	12	4	3
6	1	12	3	4
6	2	19	6	3.1
6	3	16	5	3.1

Again we will summarize the data by collapsing them, but now we have two dependent variables, each of which needs to be summarized differently. We want the mean number of symptoms and the median severity of the symptoms:

```
> collapse mean_sym=mean(#symptoms) med_sev=med(med_severity), by day
```

day	mean_sym	med_sev
1	0.0	0.0
2	1.0	1.0
3	2.7	2.0
4	3.7	2.3
5	4.0	3.0
6	4.7	3.1
etc.		

> *Two (or more) dependent variables can be collapsed at the same time.*

Two y-variables can be plotted in the same graph. One corresponds to the left y-axis and the other corresponds to the right y-axis.

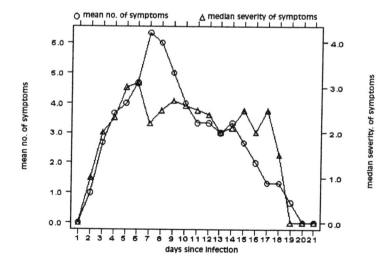

This graph gives us a more detailed picture of what's behind the earlier graphs of the cssi: a rapid increase in both symptoms and severity; a leveling off in symptoms followed by a peak in severity; a decline in severity with fairly constant symptoms until the end.

10.5 Exercises

1. Here are some data on U.S. alcohol consumption(gallons of ethanol per capita):

year	type	amount	year	type	amount
1940	beer	0.73	1970	beer	1.14
1940	wine	0.16	1970	wine	0.27
1940	spirits	0.67	1970	spirits	1.11
1950	beer	1.04	1980	beer	1.38
1950	wine	0.23	1980	wine	0.34
1950	spirits	0.77	1980	spirits	1.04
1960	beer	0.99	1990	beer	1.34
1960	wine	0.22	1990	wine	0.33
1960	spirits	0.86	1990	spirits	0.78

Collapse the data to get the total alcohol consumption for each year listed.

2. Here are some data on capital punishment:

year	race	#executed	year	race	#executed
1990	white	16	1993	white	23
1990	black	7	1993	black	14
1990	other	0	1993	other	1
1991	white	7	1994	white	20
1991	black	7	1994	black	11
1991	other	0	1994	other	0
1992	white	19	1995	white	33
1992	black	11	1995	black	22
1992	other	1	1995	other	1

a. Collapse the data to find the total number of executions in each year.
b. Collapse the data to find the mean number of prisoners of each race executed per year.

3. Suppose some memory researchers are interested in how certain aspects of words affect verbal memory. They construct a list of nouns that are either common or uncommon and either concrete or abstract. For example, here is a portion of the list:

house	{common, concrete}
love	{common, abstract}
javelin	{uncommon, concrete}
tyrant	{uncommon, abstract}

The experimenters read the list (only the words) aloud to a group of four subjects, and then immediately ask them to write down as many words as they can recall. The number of words each subject correctly recalls is recorded. A week later the subjects come back and are again asked to write down as many words as they can recall. Again the number of words each subject correctly recalls is recorded. The data might look like this:

subject	word frequency	word type	immediate recall	delayed recall
1	1	1	4	3
1	1	2	7	5
1	2	1	3	3
1	2	2	10	6
2	1	1	2	3
2	1	2	6	4
2	2	1	3	1
2	2	2	7	6
3	1	1	4	4
3	1	2	8	5
3	2	1	3	0
3	2	2	7	7
4	1	1	5	3
4	1	2	7	4
4	2	1	3	2
4	2	2	8	3
	(1=high, 2=low)	(1=abstract, 2=concrete)		

a. Collapse the data to find the mean and standard deviation of the immediate recall and the delayed recall.

b. Collapse the data to find the mean and standard deviation of the immediate recall and the delayed recall for each combination of word frequency and word type.

c. Create a new variable, change, and make its values equal to the delayed recall minus the immediate recall. (For example, the first value of change will be -1, indicating that subject 1 recalled one word less in the delayed recall than in the immediate recall.) Collapse the data to find the mean of change for each combination of word frequency and word type.

Demonstration 8

Looking at Faces, Part III

WE RETURN AGAIN to Dennis Dickinson's study of the relation between perceived attractiveness and perceived happiness. We created the data set in Demonstration 1, checked and corrected it in Demonstration 2, and now we will see what we can learn from the data.

Recall that Dennis showed photographs of 48 faces to 80 subjects; 40 rated the attractiveness of each face and the other 40 rated the happiness of each face. Each group of raters consisted of roughly equal numbers of men and women. The data set (faces.dat) contains these variables:

```
variable                values                        variable name
subject number          1-40                          subnum
subject sex             1=female, 2=male              subsex
picture number          1-48                          picnum
picture sex             1=female, 2=male              picsex
group                   1=happiness, 2=attractiveness group
rating                  1(low)-7(high)                rating
```

Dennis's original question was a simple one: Do we judge happier faces as more attractive? Do we judge more attractive faces as happier? Because we have quantitative measures of happiness and attractiveness, we can frame these questions in terms of a relation between two quantitative variables. We might begin with a scatter plot, graphing the attractiveness rating of each face against its happiness rating, like so:

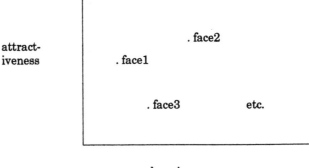

Such a graph will show us the relation, if there is one, between happiness and attractiveness. If this is what we want, the next question is: How do we make it? Looking at the variable list, two problems are apparent. First, attractiveness and happiness are not separate variables in this data set; rather, as mentioned in chapter 3, all the ratings are in the variable rating, and the variable group indicates which kind of rating a given observation contains. To make the scatter plot, therefore, we will need to restructure the data from their current scorewise organization to a casewise organization.

The second problem is that there is not one happiness rating for each face, but 40, and likewise for attractiveness. Which happiness rating for a given face should be plotted against which attractiveness rating for that face? There is no basis for pairing the two kinds of ratings, so we need to calculate a single summary value for each face for each type of rating. The usual summary measure is the mean, but remember that ratings are ordinal data, which means we are not necessarily measuring happiness and attractiveness on equal-interval scales. For example, the difference in attractiveness between two faces rated 4 and 5 may be different (probably smaller) than the difference between two faces rated 6 and 7. In these circumstances the mean may not be appropriate. In this case, however, the mean is probably acceptable, for two reasons. First, the means are very strongly correlated (r= 0.97) with the medians, the most likely alternative to the mean. Second, we are not going to be looking at any differences between means, so the fact that they come from an ordinal scale is of less importance.

We will solve the second problem first, by collapsing the individual ratings into means; specifically, the 40 happiness ratings of each face will be collapsed into a single mean, and likewise the 40 attractiveness ratings. For each face we will have not 80 ratings but two mean ratings.

```
> load file faces
> collapse meanrat=mean(rating), by picnum
```

The data set now contains 96 observations on the following:

picnum	picture number
group	rating group (happiness/attractiveness)
meanrat	mean rating

It looks like this:

picnum	picsex	group	rating
1	2	1	4.025
1	2	2	3.750
2	2	1	1.250
2	2	2	1.825
3	1	1	4.000
3	1	2	4.125
4	2	1	4.350
4	2	2	3.800
...			

These are the data we need for the scatter plot, but we have to arrange them casewise:

```
> restructure casewise / id=picnum
  / grouping var=group, values=1,2
  / dep var=meanrat, prefix=mean_
> rename mean_1, newname=mean_att
> rename mean_2, newname=mean_hap
```

Now the data set looks like this:

picnum	picsex	mean_att	mean_hap
1	male	3.750	4.025
2	male	1.825	1.250
3	female	4.025	4.000
4	male	3.800	4.350
5	male	2.875	2.075
6	female	4.275	4.825
7	female	4.400	3.000
8	male	4.150	4.350
9	female	4.325	5.075
10	male	4.500	4.425

. . .

```
> plot cases, x=mean_hap, y=mean_att
```

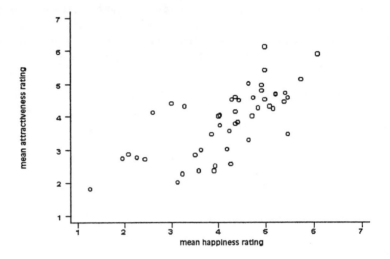

Each dot in the scatter plot represents one of the 48 faces. The shape of the cloud of dots shows that there is indeed a relation between mean happiness ratings and mean attractiveness ratings: in general, the higher a face's mean happiness rating, the higher its mean attractiveness rating, and vice versa. We can compute a correlation coefficient to get a sense of how strong the relation is:

```
> compute correlation of mean_att mean_hap
```

n = 48   r = 0.71

How should we interpret an r of .71? We can do a significance test on it, but a more useful interpretation is in terms of explained variance. r^2 is .5, which means that half of the variance in one rating can be explained by the other rating. That's pretty good, but it's hard not to wonder what might explain the other half of the variance.

The scatter plot above contains all 48 faces. Some are female and some are male, but which dots are which? Is it possible that plotting male and female faces separately would give a clearer picture of what's going on? It is, and there are two ways to do this. One is to use different plotting symbols for male and female faces:

```
> plot cases, x=mean_hap, y=mean_att, symbols are picsex(1)=f pic
  sex(2)=m
```

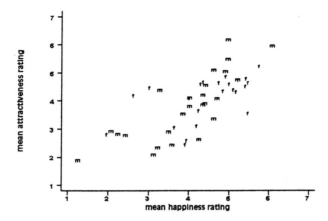

Look closely and you will see that there is a difference. The male faces show more variability with respect to both happiness and attractiveness ratings; that is, the highest and lowest mean ratings belong to male faces. Other things being equal, this would result in a higher attractiveness-happiness correlation for male faces than for female faces.

Another approach is to make separate scatter plots for male and female faces:

```
>plot cases if picsex=1, x=mean_hap, y=mean_att
```

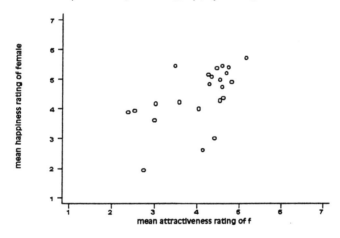

```
>plot cases if picsex=2, x=mean_hap, y=mean_att
```

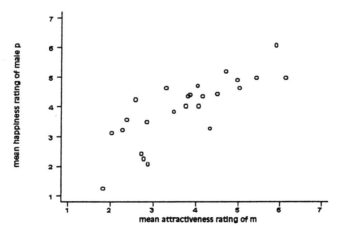

These graphs show that attractiveness and happiness are more strongly related for male faces than for female faces. The correlation coefficients bear this out:

```
> compute correlation of mean_att mean_hap if picsex=1
-> picsex=    female  n = 23  r = 0.55

> compute correlation of mean_att mean_hap if picsex=2
-> picsex=      male  n = 25  r = 0.79
```

The explained variance has dropped to 30% for the female faces and risen to 63% for the male faces. This is already an interesting result, one that might lead to some interesting speculation about why we seem to look at female and male faces differently. But who is "we"? In Dennis's experiment, "we" were female and male raters; perhaps another separation is in order. To do this we need to go back to the original data set and collapse it in a different way.

```
> load file faces
> collapse meanrat=mean(rating), by picnum picsex subsex group
```

Collapsing the data set in this way produces a mean rating for each picture for each combination of picsex, subsex, and group. There are two values for each of these variables, so there will be 2 x 2 x 2 = 8 means for each picture, but four will be missing because a given picture has only one sex. The data set now looks like this:

picnum	picsex	group	subsex	meanrat
1	male	happy	female	3.89
1	male	attract.	female	3.68
1	male	happy	male	4.14
1	male	attract.	male	3.81
2	male	happy	female	1.26
2	male	attract.	female	1.95
2	male	happy	male	1.24
2	male	attract.	male	1.71
3	female	happy	female	3.79
3	female	attract.	female	4.00
3	female	happy	male	4.19
3	female	attract.	male	4.05
...				

As before, these are the data we want to plot, but we need to put them into a casewise arrangement. The problem is that we have three independent variables (picsex, group, subsex) but we want a data set with one column of ratings for each of the eight combinations of the independent variables. We need to create a single variable with eight values, each of which will become the name of one of those columns when the data are reoriented.

```
> create temp, values=.              [set all values to missing]
> change temp=1 if group==1 & subsex==1 & picsex==1
> change temp=2 if group==1 & subsex==1 & picsex==2
> change temp=3 if group==1 & subsex==2 & picsex==1
> change temp=4 if group==1 & subsex==2 & picsex==2
> change temp=5 if group==2 & subsex==1 & picsex==1
> change temp=6 if group==2 & subsex==1 & picsex==2
```

```
> change temp=7 if group==2 & subsex==2 & picsex==1
> change temp=8 if group==2 & subsex==2 & picsex==2
```

Here's what the data set looks like:

picnum	picsex	group	subsex	temp	meanrat
1	male	happy	female	2	3.89
1	male	attract.	female	6	3.68
1	male	happy	male	4	4.14
1	male	attract.	male	8	3.81
2	male	happy	female	2	1.26
2	male	attract.	female	6	1.95
2	male	happy	male	4	1.24
2	male	attract.	male	8	1.71
3	female	happy	female	1	3.79
3	female	attract.	female	5	4.00
3	female	happy	male	3	4.19
3	female	attract.	male	7	4.05
...					

The new variable `temp` will take the place of `picsex`, `subsex`, and `group` as we rearrange the data set:

```
> restructure casewise / id=picnum
   / grouping var=temp, values=1,2,3,4,5,6,7,8
   / dep var=meanrat, prefix=mean
```

Now we have:

picnum	mean1	mean2	mean3	mean4	mean5	mean6	mean7	mean8
1	.	3.89	.	4.14	.	3.68	.	3.81
2	.	1.26	.	1.24	.	1.95	.	1.71
3	3.79	.	4.19	.	4.00	.	4.05	.
...								

The 1, 2, 3, etc. attached to mean are the values of `temp`. It would help to rename these variables:

```
> rename mean1, newname=hfpic_fs
> label hfpic_fs "mean happiness of f face by f subs"

> rename mean2, newname=hmpic_fs
> label hmpic_fs "mean happiness of m face by f subs"

> rename mean3, newname=hfpic_ms
> label hfpic_ms "mean happiness of f face by m subs"

> rename mean4, newname=hmpic_ms
> label hmpic_ms "mean happiness of m face by m subs"

> rename mean5, newname=afpic_fs
> label afpic_fs "mean attractiveness of f face by f subs"

> rename mean6, newname=ampic_fs
> label afpic_ms "mean attractiveness of f face by m subs"

> rename mean7, newname=afpic_ms
> label ampic_ms "mean attractiveness of m face by m subs"

> rename mean8, newname=ampic_ms
> label ampic_fs "mean attractiveness of m face by f subs"
```

(Because variable names must be short they can get a little cryptic. When this happens it is doubly important to label the variables.)

Finally we can make the scatter plots. Because a given picture is either female or male, it will have mean ratings in only four variables, either `hfpic_ms`, `hfpic_fs`, `afpic_ms`, and `afpic_fs` (female faces) or `hmpic_ms`, `hmpic_fs`, `ampic_ms`, and `ampic_fs` (male faces). For each group of four variables, there are 12 possible scatter plots. It is easy to make all 12 at once in a *scatter plot matrix*:

```
>plot cases, matrix of hfpic_ms, hfpic_fs, afpic_ms, afpic_fs
```

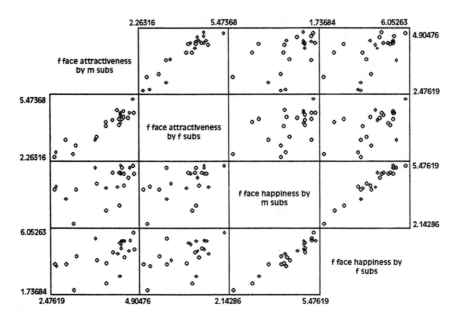

All of the dots in this matrix are female faces. Notice that men and women raters agree with one another about these faces' attractiveness and about their happiness, but that happiness ratings are only weakly related to attractiveness ratings, regardless of the sex of the rater. We might want to get some correlation coefficients to corroborate our reading of the scatter plots:

```
> compute correlation of afpic_ms afpic_fs hfpic_ms hfpic_fs
 (obs=23)
```

	afpic_ms	afpic_fs	hfpic_ms	hfpic_fs
afpic_ms	1.0000			
afpic_fs	0.9364	1.0000		
hfpic_ms	0.5314	0.5104	1.0000	
hfpic_fs	0.5552	0.5510	0.9623	1.0000

These are striking: Male and female raters explain 88% of the variance in one another's attractiveness ratings and 92% of the variance in one another's happiness ratings of female faces. By contrast, happiness ratings and attractiveness ratings explain only 26 to 31% of one another's variance.

Does the same pattern apply to the male faces?

```
>plot cases, matrix of hmpic_ms, hmpic_fs, ampic_ms, ampic_fs
```

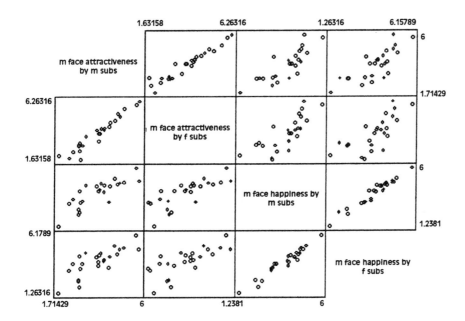

It does, but for the male faces there seems to be a somewhat stronger relation between attractiveness ratings and happiness ratings than there is for the female faces. The correlation coefficients corroborate this:

```
> compute correlation of ampic_ms ampic_fs hmpic_ms hmpic_fs
            ampic_ms    ampic_fs    hmpic_ms    hmpic_fs
--------------------------------------------------------
ampic_ms  : 1.0000
ampic_fs  : 0.9364      1.0000
hmpic_ms  : 0.5314      0.5104      1.0000
hmpic_fs  : 0.5552      0.5510      0.9623      1.0000
```

Again male and female raters explain most of the variance in one another's attractiveness (93%) and happiness (94%) ratings. But unlike the female faces, the male faces' happiness ratings and attractiveness ratings explain a fair amount (54 to 68%) of one another's variance.

Is there something different about female and male faces? Maybe. Or is there something different about the way we – men and women – look at female and male faces? Maybe. But before speculating about what these difference might be, take another look at the scatter plot matrices. The software has set up the axes to accommodate the minimum and maximum values occurring in the data (rather than the minimum and maximum possible values); this spreads the data points out over as large an area as possible, making it easier to see what's going on. Because we're most interested in the shape of the data points, it is easy to ignore the axes of a scatter plot, but when we have many scatter plots we should take note of the axes. In this case, the axes of the female faces' matrix have smaller ranges than the axes of the male faces' matrix. This raises the possibility that the difference we have observed between the correlations from the female faces' matrix and the correlations from the male faces' matrix are an artifact. Other things being equal, a correlation coefficient increases as the range of one or both variables increases. This means that we have to watch out for restriction of range (i.e., an artificial restriction of the range of one or both variables) and for outliers (i.e., data points with extreme values on one or both variables). Restriction of range will lead to an *r* that underestimates the true correlation, and outliers will produce an *r* that overestimates the true correlation. If Dennis's female faces happened to be a little more homogeneous with respect to those characteristics that are reflected in happiness and/or attractiveness ratings, then restriction of range in the female faces might explain the male/female difference. If Dennis's male faces happened to include a few that were particularly high or low in those characteristics, then these outliers might explain the male/female difference. Looking at the scatter plots, it is hard to say which is more likely, and it is quite possible that both are true.

There are a number of ways this experiment could be designed to avoid this problem next time around. Such considerations are outside the scope of this book, so I will leave the redesign of Dennis's experiment as a challenge for you. For now our concern is to learn what we can from the data we have. Here is a summary:

1. Female and male raters strongly agree with one another about the attractiveness and the happiness of the faces.

2. Overall, there is a moderate correlation between attractiveness and happiness.

3. The attractiveness/happiness correlation begins to disintegrate when we break the ratings down by sex of face and sex of rater. Specifically, it holds for male faces but not for female faces.

4a. This asymmetry may reflect an aspect of the way we look at faces or

4b. it may be an artifact of the particular stimuli used.

5. We would have missed 4b had we not carefully examined a large number of scatter plots. More than anything else, this analysis illustrates the danger of computing statistics, descriptive or inferential, without examining the data.

Demonstration 9

Sundown Syndrome

PEOPLE WHO WORK in nursing homes will tell you that the patients tend to act up when the sun goes down. My student Hortense Lynch wanted to find out whether this "sundown syndrome" is a nursing legend or an objective pattern of patient behavior. This demonstration illustrates an aspect of research that we all encounter from time to time, namely that sometimes you wind up with data that lead you in an unexpected direction.

Hortense was given access to monthly nursing records at a nursing home in the Boston area. She had two criteria in drawing her sample: (a) that the patient have records covering two years of continuous residence; and (b) that the same two-year period apply to all patients sampled. Six female residents met these requirements, and Hortense recorded the number of incidents of disruptive behavior by each patient in each of the three eight-hour nursing shifts in each month of the sample period. The nursing records noted 34 specific behaviors; Hortense selected those that were disruptive: repetitive yelling, verbal abuse (of the staff), agitation, anxiety, and physical abuse (of the staff).

The data set contains 2160 observations (6 patients x 5 behaviors x 3 shifts x 12 months x 2 years) and contains the following variables:

patient	(1 - 6)
shift	(7am-3pm; 3pm-11pm; 11pm-7am)
month	(1 - 12)
year	(1997, 1998)
behavior	(1 - 5)
incs	number of incidents

The data set is in a scorewise organization, so each row contains the number of incidents of a specific kind of disruptive behavior by one patient during one shift in one month in one year.

The sundown hypothesis predicts that there will be more incidents of disruptive behavior during the second shift (3pm - 11pm). At Boston's latitude sunset is within this shift all year round. Accordingly, we might begin by looking at the mean number of incidents (of all types) in each shift.

```
> compute mean sd of incident, by shift
```

	Summary of no. of incidents		
shift	Mean	Std.Dev.	Freq.
7am-3pm	10.0	4.7	720
3pm-11pm	12.4	5.2	720
11pm-7am	3.6	4.5	720
Total	8.7	6.1	2160

These means are consistent with the hypothesis, but we should also look at the distributions of incidents within each shift:

> plot box, x=shift, y=incs

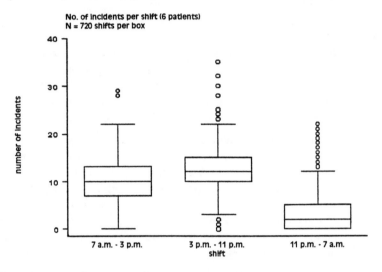

This graph shows that there is substantial overlap between the distributions for the first two shifts and that there are a few very high scores in the second shift that might have inflated the mean somewhat. Is the difference reliable? I will leave this as an exercise for you.

Even assuming that patients are significantly more disruptive during the second shift than during either of the others, the most we can say is that the data are consistent with the sundown hypothesis. The problem is that measuring time in eight-hour units is too coarse for our purposes. It's quite possible that the patients misbehaved mostly at the beginning and/or end of the second shift rather than at sundown. If we had a more fine-grained time variable we could see whether, from month to month, the peak in misbehavior corresponds to the approximate time of sundown during that month. Such data would offer a stronger test of the hypothesis, but, alas, were not available.

We might stop there, but it is hard to resist the opportunity to look around in such a nice data set. For example, we might ask whether the difference between shifts is consistent across the sample period or is an artifact of aggregating data.

An effective way to do this is to create a multiple line graph. We will plot the mean number of incidents for each shift for each month, and then connect the 12 data points in each shift. Some software will automate some or all of the data manipulations necessary to make such a graph, but we will do it by hand to learn what needs to be done.

The graph we're creating will have three separate dependent (y) variables (each shift's number of incidents) plotted against the same independent (x) variable (month). The data set, on the other hand, has one shift (grouping) variable and one incs (dependent) variable. Therefore our first step is to reorient the data so as to combine these variables.

```
> restructure casewise / id=patient,year,month,behavior
  / grouping var=shift, values=1,2,3
  / dep var=incs, prefix=incs_s
```

Now the data set looks like this:

	patient	month	year	behavior	incs_s1	incs_2	incs_3
1	1	1	1997	1	5	12	3
2	1	1	1997	2	6	12	1
3	1	1	1997	3	8	12	5
4	1	1	1997	4	7	13	4
5	1	1	1997	5	8	14	2
6	1	1	1998	1	8	10	1
7	1	1	1998	2	7	11	0
8	1	1	1998	3	8	10	2
9	1	1	1998	4	4	14	1
10	1	1	1998	5	7	15	6
11	etc.						

The next step is to reduce these 2160 observations to 36 (3 shifts x 12 months). That is, instead of a raw value of incs_s1, incs_s2, and incs_s3 for each of the 720 combinations of patient, month, year, and behavior, we want a mean value of incs_s1, incs_s2, and incs_s3 for each month.

```
> collapse mean1=mean(incs1) mean2=mean(incs2) mean3=mean(incs3), by
  month
```

The collapsed data set contains just the four variables we need for the graph:

```
month
mean1
mean2
mean3
```

```
> plot line, x=month, y=mean1, mean2, mean3
```

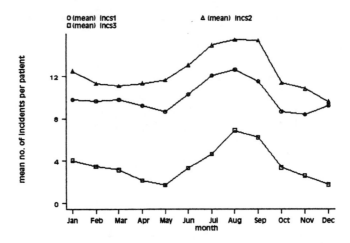

Each set of connected points is a shift. As predicted, the mean number of incidents in the second shift (top line) is consistently higher than the mean number of incidents in the first shift (middle line). There's something else here, however, that is potentially just as interesting as the difference between the shifts: incidents peak, in all three shifts, in the late summer. To get an idea of how seriously to take this pattern, we can add error bars to the graph.

Error bars usually represent either standard deviations or confidence intervals. For our present purpose confidence intervals are the more appropriate choice because we are not interested in the variability of the scores behind each data point per se, but rather in how closely these sample means estimate the true values.

A confidence interval is written as

$$(\text{mean} - z \times se) < \mu < (\text{mean} + z \times se)$$

[where z is the normal deviate corresponding to the chosen confidence level and se is the standard error of the sample mean]

which means that we are confident that the true value of the mean (μ) is somewhere within $z \times se$ of the sample mean. The higher the confidence level, the bigger z, and hence the confidence interval, will be. For a 95% confidence interval, z=1.96, which cuts off .025 in each tail of the normal curve.

To compute these intervals, we need the sample means, which we already have, and the corresponding standard errors, which we can compute from the standard deviations. Here is the same command we used before to collapse the data, but this time we are asking for standard deviations as well as means:

```
> collapse  mean1=mean(incs1)  mean2=mean(incs2)  mean3=mean(incs3)
  sd1=sd(incs1) sd2=sd(incs2) sd3=sd(incs3), by month
```

Now we compute the upper (hi) and lower (lo) boundaries of the confidence interval for each mean:

```
> create hi1, values=mean1+1.96*(sd1/sqrt(60))
> create lo1, values=mean1-1.96*(sd1/sqrt(60))
> create hi2, values=mean2+1.96*(sd2/sqrt(60))
> create lo2, values=mean2-1.96*(sd2/sqrt(60))
> create hi3, values=mean3+1.96*(sd3/sqrt(60))
> create lo3, values=mean3-1.96*(sd3/sqrt(60))
```

Finally, we can graph the means and the confidence intervals (represented as error bars)[1]:

```
>plot line, x=month, y=mean1, mean2, mean3, errorbars mean1(hi1, lo1)
 mean2(hi2, lo2) mean3(hi3, lo3)
```

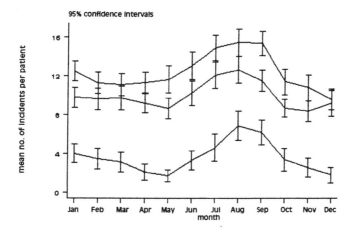

The fact that, for a given shift, the error bars around the highest means do not overlap the error bars around the lowest means suggests that there is something going on here, some kind of annual cycle of disruptiveness. (To test this suspicion more rigorously we would use trend analysis.)

Before speculating about this cycle, it would be wise to see if the same pattern emerges when the data are aggregated in different ways. For example, in the graph above, data from two years are aggregated; what if we look at the two years separately?

To do this we need to repeat the procedure we just followed, but breaking the data down by year rather than by shift. Try it – you should get something like this:

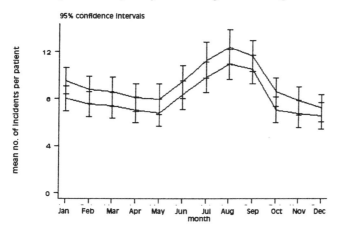

The error bars from one year overlap those of the other year, but again there is no overlap of error bars around the highest and lowest months in each year – the pattern persists.

What about the different categories of behavior? Again, the same procedure leads to:

---

[1] Some software will produce error-bar graphs from un-aggregated data, automatically carrying out the steps we've gone through.

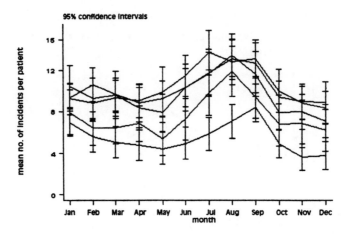

Still the pattern persists. This graph also makes the point that there is a limit to how many overlapping error bars should appear in one graph. What that limit is may vary, but we have certainly exceeded it here. One solution is to plot each line separately:

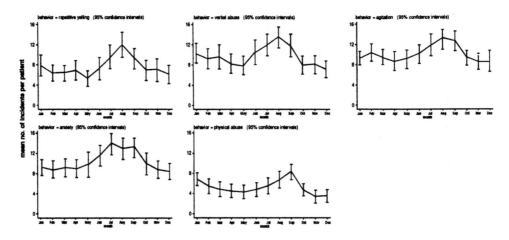

Has Hortense discovered something new about nursing home patients? Or is there a less exciting explanation for these data? It's hard to say, but there are several possibilities that we can't rule out with the present data. For example, is there some annual staff turnover or reassignment that might explain the summertime increase in disruptive behaviors? Are there summer employees who either elicit disruptive behavior or who increase the proportion of disruptive behavior that gets recorded? Is there a seasonal change in the number of visitors? Is it simply the heat?

To rule out such explanations Hortense will need to collect more data from other patients and from other nursing homes. What she finds may ultimately shed some light on her original question about sundown syndrome, but what is important from our point of view is that she would have missed an interesting puzzle if she hadn't explored her data.

Appendix A: Popular Software Equivalents of Pseudocode Commands

Task	Pseudocode	SPSS	Stata	Remarks
Append a data set	append file *filename*	Data - Merge Files - Add Cases	append using *filename*	
Bar graph	plot bar, x=*groupvar*, y=*var*	Graphs - Bar	graph *yvar*, bar mean by(*xvar*)	
Box-and-whisker plot	plot box, x=*groupvar*, y=*var*	Graphs - Boxplot	graph *yvar*, box by(*xvar*)	
Change the values of a variable	change *var* to *expression*	Transform - Compute	replace *var* = *expression*	
Collapse	collapse *newvar* = *func*(*var*), by *varlist*	Data - Aggregate	collapse [see manual]	
Correlate	compute correlation of *varlist*	Statistics - Correlate - Bivariate	correlate *varlist*	If more than two variables are named, the results will be displayed in a correlation matrix.
Delete a case or cases	delete rows *range*	click on row nos. in data editor; press <del> key	drop in *range*	
Delete a variable	delete *var*	click on var. name in data editor; press <del> key	drop *var*	
Descriptive statistics - see Summarize				

Task	Pseudocode	SPSS	Stata	Remark
Encode the values of a string var.	encode *var* into *newvar*	Transform - Automatic Recode	encode *var*, generate(*newvar*)	
Label a variable	label *var* "*label*"	Data - Define Variable - Labels — enter variable label	label variable *var* "*label*"	
Label the values of a variable	label *var* values 1= , 2= , etc.	Data - Define Variable - Labels — enter value labels	step 1: label define *labelname* 1= , 2= , etc. step 2: label value *var labelname*	
Line graph	plot line, x=*seriesvar*, y=*var*	Graphs - Line	graph *yvar xvar*, connect(l)	
List some data	list *varlist*	use data editor	list *varlist* (or use data editor)	
Load a data file (native format)	load file *filename*	File - Open	use *filename*	
Load a data file (text format)	read file *filename*, vars are *varlist*	File - Read ASCII Data	infile *varlist* using(*filename*)	
Merge two data sets, 1-to-1	merge file *filename*	Data - Merge Files - Add Variables	merge using *filename*	
Merge two data sets, matching cases	merge file *filename*, match on *varlist*	Data - Merge Files - Add Variables — select match in dialog box	merge *matchvar(s)* using *filename*	
Missing value (system) symbol				
New variable	create *newvar*, values=*expression*	step 1: Data - Define Variable step 2: Transform - Compute	generate *newvar* = *expression*	

Task	Pseudocode	SPSS	Stata	Remark
Rearrange a data set	restructure scorewise... restructure casewise...	must do this by hand in data editor	reshape [see manual]	SPSS Transpose merely exchanges row and columns.
Rename a variable	rename *var*, newname=*newname*	double click on name of variable in data editor	rename *var newname*	
Save a data file	save file *filename*	File - Save / Save As	save *filename*	
Scatter plot	plot cases, x=*xvar*, y=*yvar*	Graphs - Scatter	graph *yvar xvar*	
Sort	sort on *varlist*, ascending/descending	Data - Sort Cases	gsort +/- *varlist*	
Summarize a quantitative variable	compute mean sd of *var*	Statistics - Summarize - Descriptives	summ *var*	
Summarize a quantitative variable, 1 by-variable	compute mean sd of *var*, by *var*	Statistics - Custom Tables - Basic Tables -or- Statistics - Compare Means - Means	tabulate *catvar*, summ(*quantvar*)	
Summarize a quantitative variable, 2 by-variables	compute mean sd of *var*, by *varlist*	Statistics - Custom Tables - Basic Tables	tabulate *catvar*, summ(*quantvar*)	
Tabulate 1 categorical variable	tabulate row=*var*	Statistics - Summarize - Frequencies	tabulate *var*	
Tabulate 2 categorical variables	tabulate row=var, col=var	Statistics - Summarize - Crosstabs	tabulate *rowvar colvar*	

Task	Pseudocode	SPSS	Stata	Remark
Tabulate 3 categorical variables	tabulate row=*var*, col=*var*, by *var*	Statistics - Custom Tables - General Tables	table *rowvar colvar byvar* c(*freq*)	
t-test, independent	compute t (unpaired) *var1* = *var2*	not possible	ttest *var1* = *var2*, unpaired	for casewise data
t-test, independent	compute t (unpaired) *dvar*, groups are *groupvar* = *val1*, *val2*	Statistics - Compare Means - Independent Samples T Test	ttest *dvar*, by(*groupvar*)	for scorewise data
t-test, paired	compute t (paired) *var1* = *var2*	Statistics - Compare Means - Paired Samples T Test	ttest *var1* = *var2*	for casewise data

Appendix B: Descriptions of Data Files

All data files referred to in the text are on the Allyn & Bacon web site (www.abacon.com/miller). These files are in plain ASCII format so that they can be used with any statistical software by using that software's equivalent of the `load file` command (see Appendix A).

file name	variables name	description	values
alcohol.txt (11 cases)	region	region	string
	alcohol	per capita alcohol expenditures (£/week)	numeric
	tobacco	per capita tobacco expenditures (£/week)	numeric
cereals.txt (77 cases)	name	name of cereal	string(35)
	mfr	manufacturer	string(1)
			A=American Home Food Products
			G=General Mills
			K=Kelloggs
			N=Nabisco
			P=Post
			Q=Quaker Oats
			R=Ralston Purina
	type	cereal type	string(1)
			C = cold
			H = hot
	calories	calories per serving	numeric
	protein	protein (g) per serving	numeric
	fat	fat (g) per serving	numeric
	sodium	sodium (mg) per serving	numeric
	fiber	dietary fiber (g) per serving	numeric
	carbo	complex carbohydrates (g) per serving	numeric
	sugars	sugars (g) per serving	numeric
	potass	potassium (mg) per serving	numeric
	vitamins	vitamins/minerals - typ. % rda	numeric
	shelf	display shelf (counting from floor)	numeric
	weight	weight (oz.) of one serving	numeric
	volume	volume (cups) of one serving	numeric

variables

file name	name	description	values
crime1.txt (10000 cases)	year	year of report	numeric
	month	month of report	numeric 1=January... 12=December
	day	day of report	numeric (1..31)
	time	time of report (24-hour clock)	numeric
	filenum	EWPD file number	numeric
	offense	type of offense	numeric 1=public nuisance
			2=robbery
			3=assault
			4=rape
			5=murder
			6=theft
			7=vandalism
			8=fraud
			9=other
	arrests	number of arrests made	numeric
	status	status of case	numeric 1=under active investigation
			2=unsolved, inactive
			3=investigation completed
			9=other
crime2.txt (10000 cases)	{same as crime1.txt, but without errors}		
cuckoo.txt (120 cases)	m_pipit	cuckoo egg lng. (mm) in meadow pipit nest	numeric
	t_pipit	cuckoo egg lng. (mm) in tree pipit nest	numeric
	h_spar	cuckoo egg lng. (mm) in hedge sparrow nest	numeric
	robin	cuckoo egg lng. (mm) in robin nest	numeric
	p_wagt	cuckoo egg lng. (mm) in pied wagtail nest	numeric
	wren	cuckoo egg lng. (mm) in wren nest	numeric

variables

file name	name	description	values
faces1.txt (3840 cases)	subnum	subject number	numeric
	subsex	subject sex	numeric 1=female 2=male
	picnum	picture number	numeric
	picsex	picture sex	numeric 1=female 2=male
	group	rating group	numeric 1=happiness 2=attractiveness
	rating	rating (1=low, 7=high)	numeric
faces2.txt (3840 cases)	[same as faces1.txt, but all errors have been corrected]		
fusion.txt (78 cases)	time	fusion time (sec.)	numeric
	group	group	numeric 1=did not see object 2=saw object
gloves.txt (23 cases)	period	observation period	numeric 1=before intervention 2=one month after intervention 3=two months after 4=5 months after intervention
	observed	number of times the nurse was observed	numeric
	gloves	number of times the nurse used gloves	numeric
	experience	years of experience of nurse	numeric

variables

file name	name	description	values
homerun1.txt (163 cases)	game	game number	numeric (1-163)
	day	days since beginning of season	numeric
	location	game location	numeric 0=away 1=home
	c_runs	runs scored by Cardinals	numeric
	o_runs	runs scored by opponent	numeric
	h_runs	home runs hit by McGwire	numeric
	rbi	runs driven in by McGwire's home runs	numeric
	status	McGwire's game status	numeric 0=played 1=didn't play
homerun2.txt (163 cases)	game	game number	numeric (1-163)
	day	days since beginning of season	numeric
	location	game location	numeric 0=away 1=home
	c_runs	runs scored by Cubs	numeric
	o_runs	runs scored by opponent	numeric
	h_runs	home runs hit by Sosa	numeric
	rbi	runs driven in by Sosa's home runs	numeric
	status	Sosa's game status	numeric 0=played 1=didn't play

variables

file name	name	description	values
kids.txt (478 cases)	gender	gender of student	string ("boy" or "girl")
	grade	grade of student	numeric 4, 5 or 6
	age	age of student in years	numeric
	race	race of student	string ("white" or "other")
	area	type of area	string ("rural", "suburban", or "urban")
	school	name of school	string
	goals	choice in personal goals question	numeric 1=make good grades 2=be popular 3=be good in sports
	grades	rank of "make good grades"	numeric 1 - 4
	sports	rank of "being good at sports"	numeric 1 - 4
	looks	rank of "being handsome or pretty"	numeric 1 - 4
	money	rank of "having lots of money"	numeric 1 - 4
olympics.txt (20 cases)	highjump	height of highest high jump (inches)	numeric
	discus	distance of longest discus throw (inches)	numeric
	longjump	distance of longest long jump (inches)	numeric
	year	Oympic year	numeric
planets.txt (9 cases)	planet	name of planet	string
	dist_sun	avg. distance from sun (millions of miles)	numeric
	orbit	duration of orbit (earth days)	numeric

variables

file name	name	description	values
poverty.txt (97 cases)	birth	Live birth rate per 1,000 of population	numeric
	death	Death rate per 1,000 of population	numeric
	infdeath	Infant deaths/1,000 of pop. < 1 year old	numeric
	leb_m	Life expectancy at birth for males	numeric
	leb_f	Life expectancy at birth for females	numeric
	gnp	Gross National Product per capita in $US	numeric
	country	name of country	string
reading.txt (66 cases)	subject	subject number	numeric
	group	type of instruction student received	string (Basal, DRTA, or Strat)
	pre1	pretest score on 1st comp. measure	numeric
	pre2	pretest score on 2nd comp. measure	numeric
	post1	posttest score on 1st comp. measure	numeric
	post2	posttest score on 2nd comp. measure	numeric
	post3	posttest score on 3rd comp. measure	numeric
sundown.txt (2160 cases)	patient	patient number	numeric
	year	calendar year	numeric (1997, 1998)
	month	month	numeric 1=January... 12=December
	shift	nursing shift	numeric 1=7am-3pm 2=3pm-11pm 3=11pm-7am
	behavior	type of behavior	numeric 1= repeated yelling 2=verbal abuse 3=agitated 4=anxious 5=physical abuse
	incident	no. of incidents recorded	numeric

variables

file name	name	description	values
termites.txt (16 cases)	dish	dish number	numeric
	dose	amount of resin (mg)	numeric (5 or 10)
	day1	number of termites alive on 1st day	numeric
	day2	number of termites alive on 2nd day	numeric
	day3	number of termites alive on 3rd day	numeric
	day4	number of termites alive on 4th day	numeric
	day5	number of termites alive on 5th day	numeric
	day6	number of termites alive on 6th day	numeric
	day7	number of termites alive on 7th day	numeric
	day8	number of termites alive on 8th day	numeric
	day9	number of termites alive on 9th day	numeric
	day10	number of termites alive on 10th day	numeric
	day11	number of termites alive on 11th day	numeric
	day12	number of termites alive on 12th day	numeric
	day13	number of termites alive on 13th day	numeric
	day14	number of termites alive on 14th day	numeric
	day15	number of termites alive on 15th day	numeric
tv.txt (40 cases)	country	name of country	string
	life	life expectancy	numeric
	pptv	people per television	numeric
	ppp	people per physician	numeric
	f_life	female life expectancy	numeric
	m_life	male life expectancy	numeric
waste.txt (95 cases)	waste_p1	weekly % waste rel. to computer, Plant 1	numeric
	waste_p2	weekly % waste rel. to computer, Plant 2	numeric
	waste_p3	weekly % waste rel. to computer, Plant 3	numeric
	waste_p4	weekly % waste rel. to computer, Plant 4	numeric
	waste_p5	weekly % waste rel. to computer, Plant 5	numeric

REFERENCES

Baumann, J. F., Seifert-Kessell, N., and Jones, L. A. (1989). Reading comprehension study. Unpublished report, Purdue University.

Central Statistical Office (1981). *Family spending*. London: HMSO

Chase, M.A., and Dummer, G.M. (1992). The role of sports as a social determinant for children. *Research Quarterly for Exercise and Sport, 63*, 418-424.

Friedland, L. R., Joffe, M., Wiley, J. F., Shapire, A., and Moore, D., et al. (1992). Effect of educational program on compliance with glove use in a pediatric emergency department. *American Journal of Diseases of Childhood, 146*, 1355-1358.

Frisby, J. P. and Clatworthy, J.L. (1975). Learning to see complex random-dot stere-grams. *Perception, 4*, 173-178.

Koopmans, L. (1987) *Introduction to Contemporary Statistical Methods* (2nd ed.). Boston: Duxbury Press.

Latter, O.H. (1902). The egg of *cuculus canorus*. *Biometrika 1*, 164.

Meinwald, J., and Messer, A. (1990). Anti-insectan compounds from the tropical tree family *Dipterocarpaceae*: Final report. Report to U. S. Agency for International Development.

Rossman, A. J. (1994). Televisions, physicians, and life expectancy. *Journal of Statistics Education* [Online], *2(1)*. Available: http://www.amstat.org/publications/jse/v2n2/datasets.rossman.html [1999, July 20].

Rouncefield, M. (1995). The statistics of poverty and inequality. *Journal of Statistics Education* [Online], *3*. Available: http://www.amstat.org/publications/jse/v3n2/datasets.rouncefield.html [1999, July 20].

Simonoff, J. S. (1998). Move over, Roger Maris: Breaking baseball's most famous record. *Journal of Statistics Education* [Online], *6*. Available: http://www.amstat.org/publications/jse/v6n3/datasets.simonoff.html [1999, July 20].

Tukey, J.W. (1977). *Exploratory data analysis*. Reading, MA: Addison-Wesley.

Winer, B.J. (1971). *Statistical principles in experimental design* (2nd ed.). New York: McGraw-Hill.

INDEX